VEGAN CUISINE

Vivian Cate

WESTBOW PRESS
A DIVISION OF THOMAS NELSON
& ZONDERVAN

Copyright © 2014 Vivian D. Cate.

All rights reserved. No part of this book may be used or reproduced by any means, graphic, electronic, or mechanical, including photocopying, recording, taping or by any information storage retrieval system without the written permission of the publisher except in the case of brief quotations embodied in critical articles and reviews.

WestBow Press books may be ordered through booksellers or by contacting:

WestBow Press
A Division of Thomas Nelson & Zondervan
1663 Liberty Drive
Bloomington, IN 47403
www.westbowpress.com
1 (866) 928-1240

Because of the dynamic nature of the Internet, any web addresses or links contained in this book may have changed since publication and may no longer be valid. The views expressed in this work are solely those of the author and do not necessarily reflect the views of the publisher, and the publisher hereby disclaims any responsibility for them.

Any people depicted in stock imagery provided by Thinkstock are models, and such images are being used for illustrative purposes only.
Certain stock imagery © Thinkstock.

ISBN: 978-1-4908-5583-7 (sc)

Library of Congress Control Number: 2014918300

Printed in the United States of America.

WestBow Press rev. date: 10/20/2014

Contents

Acknowledgements xi

INTRODUCTION 1
1. What Caused Us to Change? 3
2. You Don't Eat Meat? But How? 7
3. The Plant Based Diet 9
4. Substitutions and Tips 15
5. Sample Weekly Meal Plan 18

APPETIZERS 23
1. Chik-N-Salad Dip 25
2. Cream Cheese Celery Stuffing 25
3. Cucumber Dip 26
4. Fruit and Nut Energy Bars 26
5. Guacamole 27
6. Pepperoni Dip 28
7. Spinach Dip 28

BEVERAGES 29
1. Bob's Thirst Quenching Tea 31
2. Coconut Pineapple Smoothie 31
3. Fruit Tea 32
4. Hot Spiced Tea 32
5. Nanoberry Smoothies 33

BREADS & CEREALS 35
1. Bob's Biscuits 37
2. Fried Green Tomatoes 37
3. Bob's Whole Wheat Pancakes 38
4. Cornbread 39
5. Granola 39

6. Joanie's Dressing 40
7. Momma's Christmas Sweet Rolls 41
8. Sweet Potato Muffins 42

DESSERTS 43
1. Almond Peach Pie 45
2. Annie Lucenia's Apple Pie 46
3. Chia Pudding 47
4. Chia Banana Pudding 47
5. Chia Pie 48
6. Key Lime Chia Pie 48
7. Ice Cream 48
8. Pumpkin Pie 49
9. Ryan's Pineapple Upside Down Cake 50
10. Strawberry Rhubarb Pie 51

ENTREES 53
1. Barbecue "Chicken" 55
2. Black-eyed Pea Veggie Casserole 55
3. Bob's Sweet and Sour Chicken 56
4. Bumble Bean Stew 56
5. Chik-N-Salad 57
6. Chili & Chili Enchiladas 58
7. Delicious Pot Pies 59
8. Eggplant Spaghetti 61
9. Freezer Friendly Family Favorite Fagioli 61
10. Italian Sausage Casserole 62
11. Lentil Chili 63
12. Macaroni and Cheese 64
13. Meatless Loaf with Sauce 66
14. Omelet 67
15. Quesadillas 68
16. Tomato Quiche 69

17. Quinoa "Chicken" Stir Fry 70
18. Rock Island Jambalaya 70
19. Sausage and Kraut 71
20. Sausage Patties 72
21. Stir Fry (Basic, Oriental, and Spaghetti) 73
22. Stroganoff 74
23. Stuffed Green Peppers 75
24. Taco Cabbage and "Beef" Casserole 75
25. Taco "Chicken" and Rice Casserole 76
26. Tasty Tortilla Stack 77
27. Traditional Spaghetti 78

FRUIT SIDE DISHES 79
1. Cranberry Relish 81
2. Fruit Salad 81
3. Granny's Favorite Ambrosia 82
4. Pappy's Pear and Peanut Butter Side Dish 83
5. Peach Chutney 84

SALADS & DRESSINGS 85
1. Chef Salads 87
2. Chinese Coleslaw 88
3. Four Bean Salad 88
4. Garbanzo Bean Salad 89
5. Mandarin Quinoa Salad 90
6. Noodled Garden Salad 90
7. Orzo Salad 91
8. Pasta Vegetable Salad 92
9. Pineapple Coleslaw 93
10. Pomegranate Bean Salad 93
11. Seitan Salad Stuffed Tomatoes 94
12. Taco Salad 94
13. Vegetable Couscous Salad 95

14.	Barbeque French Dressing	96
15.	Cucumber Dressing	97
16.	French Dressing	97
17.	Red Wine Vinegar Dressing	98
18.	Vivian's Ranch Dressing	98

SANDWICHES 101

1.	American Grilled Burgers	103
2.	BLT Sandwich	103
3.	Bumble Bean Burritos	104
4.	Chik-N-Salad Sandwich	105
5.	Cucumber Spread Sandwich	105
6.	Eggless Salad Sandwich	106
7.	Lemon Cumato Sandwich	106
8.	Meatless Loaf Sandwich	107
9.	OLT Sandwich	108
10.	Pig in a Blanket with Mustard Sauce	109
11.	Pimento Cheese Sandwich	109
12.	Sausage Wraps	110
13.	Sloppy Joes	110
14.	Spinach Burgers	111
15.	Stir Fry Burgers or Burritos	111

SOUPS 113

1.	Amanda's Taco Soup	115
2.	Broccoli Soup	116
3.	Butternut Squash Soup	116
4.	Cashew Cream	117
5.	"Chicken" Vegetable Soup	117
6.	Creamy Curried Potato Soup	118
7.	Hearty Soup	119
8.	Mushroom Soup	119

9.	Split Pea Soup	120
10.	Tortilla Soup	121

VEGETABLE SIDE DISHES 123
1.	Asparagus Risotto	125
2.	Baked Summer Squash	126
3.	Basil Zucchini	126
4.	Beverly's Cinnamon Sweet Potatoes	127
5.	Broccoli Casserole	127
6.	Butternut Succotash	128
7.	Can't Believe It's Turnips	128
8.	Cauli-Bean Mash	129
9.	Cheese Grits Casserole	130
10.	Creamed Spinach Over Pasta	130
11.	Gluten Free Mushroom Noodles	131
12.	Grilled Vegetables	132
13.	Jalapeno Mashed Sweet Potatoes	133
14.	Joan's Marinated Carrots	133
15.	Kale Medley	134
16.	Potato Casserole	135

ADDITIONAL INFORMATION 137
1.	Healthy Body, Healthy Soul	139
2.	Suggested Resources	143
3.	Grocery List	145
4.	Sample Monthly Meal Plan	146
5.	Monthly Meal Plan	147

Acknowledgements

*It is impossible to express my heart's gratitude to **Abba Father** for all He has done in the 64 years of my life. He is truly faithful. He is a just God, but He is so merciful. May He alone be honored in this book!*

***Bob Cate**, you have been my number one guinea pig ... from the "minus 3" you gave me for fried squid (or were they rubber bands?) many years ago to the five stars you have given several of these recipes! Thank you, Honey, for sticking with me through the joys and challenges of thirty years in marriage! I love you, my faithful and loving man!*

***Ryan Cate**, my athletic wonder and overcomer, you bring joy and laughter to our home! You are such a caring young man. Continue to grow in stature and strength before God and man, knowing that Father God has a plan for you, a plan for a future and a hope. I love you, my son, from now unto eternity!*

***Nick Cate**, my warrior, you have more abilities than a snake has scales! Leader, public speaker, power force and team player (how I love to watch you play rugby!) I am so glad you are our son! God has used you mightily in my life. May His will be done in and through you as it is in heaven. I love you forever!*

***Amanda Cate**, daughter of my heart, I enjoy being your "step-monster!" You taught me to move beyond my selfishness and to love as God loves! Dad gave you Rip Esselstyn's book and you took off on your own healthy path! What fun it has been to share recipes (one of yours is in this book) and restaurants like Wild Cow and Sunflower! I love you!*

*My deep appreciation goes to those of you who have tasted and critiqued recipes and have encouraged me to put them into a book! Specifically, **Phil and Laurie Perkins**, you have* come to the Cate "Bed and Breakfast" every spring, never knowing what would be on the menu! How I have enjoyed the many hours editing Laurie's books of fiction while Phil tinkered with our computers! Thank you, dear friends, for joyfully eating our Vegan Cuisine and then editing my first book!

Martha Neville, you are the most faithful friend (next to Jesus and my hubby, of course) that a woman could ask for. Almost every week since your Blake's sudden change of address (when he went to live with Jesus) you have eaten at our table on Wednesdays and partaken of our Sunday Samplers. Not only have you prayed for me through storms and peaceful rivers, but you have also been a great sport as Bob and I chartered the unknown waters of "veganization!"

In conclusion, I want to acknowledge the staff at Westbow Publishing! If I attempt to list names I will undoubtedly leave out someone important. However, you know who you are! You are the wonderful team of professionals who patiently (and with clarity) gave me a crash course in publishing and helped make this dream come true! Thank you!

Recipes on Front Cover

Starting with the burger and moving clockwise:

1. American Grilled Burger
2. Hearty Soup
3. Chik-N-Salad
4. Four Bean Salad
5. Mandarin Quinoa Salad
6. Chinese Coleslaw
7. Bob's Whole Wheat Pancakes
8. Fruit table (not a recipe)
9. Meatless Loaf with Sauce
10. Cucumber Dip
11. Cream Cheese Celery Stuffing
12. Fruit and Nut Energy Bars

Center recipes

1. Kale Medley (with Hominy)
2. Basil Zucchini

INTRODUCTION

What Caused Us to Change?

Several years ago my husband stopped by our local Whole Foods store. As he entered through a side door, Bob noticed a movie playing in the small education center. "Forks Over Knives" was a new video documentary, backed by scientific research, empowering people to live healthier lives. Their premise: elimination of animal products from diets, and solely eating plant based foods. That film was the beginning of a life-changing experience for both of us!

Prior to our marriage in 1984, Bob often grilled as many as 200 steaks for a local horsemen's association. Later, he cooked for a Cub Scout family camp each summer. Then he became one of three Quartermasters for a Boy Scout troop. One of their midweek meals at summer camp was grilled steak ... which Bob cooked!

My husband was a dyed-in-the-wool, till-death-do-us-part MEAT EATER! Whenever I tried a vegetarian meal, Bob wanted meat to go with it! All that changed the fateful day when my dear hubby purchased *The Engine 2 Diet* by Rip Esselstyn and came home with news that he was no longer going to eat meat!

"Yeah, right!" I exclaimed. "And what do I do with the $500 worth of meat stored in our freezer?"

Understand that my mother instilled in me a motto that I fiercely live by: "Waste not, want not!" I tried to convince Bob that we could start this new way of eating AFTER we ate up all the meat in the freezer, but he was not to be moved.

"YOU can eat it, but I am not eating any more meat," he responded.

Bob had gained at least sixty pounds since our wedding. Furthermore, his snoring had become so loud that I could hear it at the other end of our home. I'd slept with my ears plugged for fifteen years. Bob was also having periods of apnea while he slept. He stopped breathing fifteen to thirty seconds every minute. Bob's doctor informed him that his blood pressure was elevated. To make matters worse, for as long as I'd known him, Bob had frequent debilitating migraines.

I had mixed emotions about this new venture. While I was very concerned about Bob's health and excited about the prospect of eating healthier foods, I was nervous about the change. After all, we're in our 60's! Besides, what was I to do with all that stored food (I kept going over this in my mind!)

The Engine 2 Diet made the change easy. One chapter lists what to get rid of while another itemizes basic supplies needed. Methodically I started cleaning out my pantry, refrigerator, and freezer. Interestingly, God showed me creative ways to distribute this food! The hospice where I worked collected food for patients in need, so I donated all the dry goods to them. The women at my home church, West End Community, collected freezer meals for folks to utilize as needs arose. One Saturday, I baked a roast and cooked several pans of spaghetti and casseroles while Bob grilled hamburgers and chicken. Our son Ryan joined in the fun by loading these into the church freezer Sunday morning! Nothing was wasted!

Meanwhile, Bob and I began our investigation. Whole Foods, Kroger, and other stores have plenty of vegan items! In fact, I remember telling Wilbur, Bob's brother, about our new way of eating.

"I don't know if I can give up my ice cream!" Wilbur remarked.

I immediately gave him two or three samples of vegan ice cream! Soon afterwards, Bob stopped by the store, loaded up with basic vegan items, and delivered them to his brother! I don't think he was converted, but at least he had an idea of the delicious options available for those who choose a plant based diet.

Vegan Cuisine

Surprisingly, we are able to continue drinking milk (we prefer vanilla almond milk), eating ice cream (Almond Bites are our favorite), using mayonnaise (we recommend Vegenaise) and butter (Earth Balance soy free), munching on sausage (Boca links and Lightlife Gimme Lean sausage), adding sour cream and cream cheese to meals (Tofutti brands), and even chomping down a loaded fried "chicken" or vegie burger (Boca).

Do we miss meat? No way! Once we got started, we learned to "veganize" old recipes and create new ones. We substitute almond milk for cow's milk and Ener-G Egg Replacer for eggs. We made "chicken salad" with seitan or chick peas and egg salad with tofu. We dined on awesome coleslaw, delicious vegan spaghetti, potato casserole that melts in your mouth, and many other items that you'll get to enjoy as you read this book!

Did we notice any results from our new way of eating? First of all, there was no increase in our food bill. Secondly, within nine months, Bob lost fifty pounds to my thirty and was back in his wedding suit! As a result, Bob rarely snored (and I discarded the ear plugs), his sleep apnea disappeared, and his blood pressure went back to normal range. More importantly, Bob no longer had migraines!

My health improved as well. For many years, every October and March, I developed sinus infections that led to lung congestion and often pneumonia. Despite air purifiers and humidifiers running 24/7, these infections took weeks and sometimes months to resolve. Since our dietary changes, I have only had a few minor sinus irritations (generally due to dry heat when I forgot to fill the humidifier!)

Bob and I are not the only ones who have seen significant health changes. A coworker and nurse practitioner started the Vegan way of eating and, in addition to losing quite a bit of weight, she watched her Triglycerides drop from 501 to 194, and her LDLs from about 128 to 88. Those are pretty exciting results!

Many benefits of a plant based diet are not as visible... like decreased plaque in our arteries, lower cholesterol levels, and less risk of cancer, diabetes, and heart disease. However, one of my favorite results is the joy of experimenting and developing new recipes with my husband! We also love showing the "Forks Over Knives" video and preparing a buffet of assorted vegan dishes for dinner guests! Needless to say, the dietary change Bob and I made not only improved our health, but it also opened doors for fun and fellowship with others!

You Don't Eat Meat? But How?

When we tell people of our vegan or plant based diet, many seem shocked! Their first questions sound something like this, "You don't eat meat? But how do you get enough protein? And how can you possibly get the right kind of protein? Do you just eat salads?"

Interestingly, we get more nutritional variety in our diet now than we ever imagined. We learned that meat does not have the fiber needed to clean out our digestive systems. We found out fruits and vegetables not only have fiber, but they also have all types of phytonutrients not found in meat. These phytonutrients are what help our bodies fight diseases such as diabetes, cancer, and heart disease. They strengthen our immune system, helping us fight off diseases.

According to *Web*MD (www.webmd.com), protein needs vary according to age. A baby should get 10 grams a day while teenagers need 46 grams (girls) to 52 grams (boys) a day. Adult men should consume 56 grams of protein daily while adult women need 46 grams (71 grams if pregnant or breastfeeding).

Meanwhile, protein comes in all shapes and sizes, including, but not limited to, the following:

Food	Protein	Fiber	Iron
2 slices Roman Meal bread	6g	3g (10%)	10%
1 Kroger Whole Wheat Tortilla	4g	3g (10%)	8%
½ c canned mushrooms	3g	2g (8%)	6%
2 Tbsp. peanut butter	8g	2g (9%)	4%
½ c canned kidney beans	8g	5g (22%)	10%
1 c. black eyed peas	13g	11g (45%)	25%
1/3 c. seitan (wheat protein)	21g	1g (4%)	8%
½ c. canned chick peas	6g	6g (26%)	8%
½ c. canned tomatoes	1g	1g (4%)	4%

½ lb sweet potato	4.5g	8g (29%)	9%
¼ lb cauliflower	2g	3g (10%)	2%
1 medium ear sweet corn	4g	2g (8%)	2%
1 medium stalk broccoli	4g	3g (12%)	6%
Fruits (most)	1g	4-24%	2-4%
1 c. corn pasta	3.68g	27%	2%
2 oz. dry quinoa pasta	4g	16%	9%
140g. Whole wheat pasta	7.42g	25%	8%
1c. quinoa	22.27g	40%	87%
1c pearl barley	3.55g	24%	12%

While the amounts of protein in items like tomatoes are not a sufficient source of protein, when you eat such a large variety of fruits and vegetables every day, it adds up!

Compare with these meats:

Food	**Protein**	**Fiber**	**Iron**
68g beef	20g	-0-	25%
140g chicken	35g	-0-	8%

This information came from labels on packages or cans.

The Plant Based Diet

What is the difference between vegan and vegetarian? Basically, vegetarians do not eat most meats, but they might eat fish, eggs, cheese, and other milk products. Meanwhile, vegans eat no meat or animal products. This means no mayonnaise that contains eggs, no foods that contain animal milk or even casein that comes from milk.

Why would anyone choose to eliminate animal products from their diets, to eat nothing but plant based foods? Let's briefly look at it from several points of view:

Biblical Perspective

In the beginning … God. He is the one Who created the earth and all that is in it. God made the birds of the air, fish of the sea, animals, other land creatures, and man to walk in union with Him. In the beginning, man did not kill animals or eat meat. God provided plenty of fruits and vegetables, seeds and nuts for a healthy, well-balanced diet (see Genesis 1:29-30).

Then God said, "I give you every seed-bearing plant on the face of the whole earth and every tree that has fruit with seed in it. They will be yours for food. (Genesis 1:29-30 NIV)

Adam and Eve had the incredible privilege of walking with God in the Garden of Eden. Even so, they rebelled against the authority of God, and sin came into the world. That is when the blood sacrifice was started. Animals were first killed in order to cover the nakedness or sin of Adam and Eve (see Genesis 3:21 NIV).

Moving forward, scripture describes what should and should not be eaten (see *What the Bible Says About Healthy Living* by Dr. Rex Russell). For instance, we are not to eat the meat of shellfish or pigs. Why? Because they are scavengers, they eat garbage. Think about what goes into their mouths ... mercury and other toxins, decayed and leftover foods, and so on. That, in turn, goes into our bodies.

Scientific Data

Meat has no fiber, which helps move food through the digestive system and prevents constipation. Meat also has no phytonutrients while vegetables, fruits, legumes, seeds and nuts provide a plethora of phytonutrients needed to prevent disease and provide optimal health. Note that some foods appear to be meat and dairy-free but actually contain casein. A protein found in cow's milk, casein has been linked to cancer.

Cattle, chickens, and fish are often given large amounts of antibiotics and/or steroids. Consider how ingesting these medicine-laced animal products can affect humans. MSG, a flavor enhancer added to some canned foods and processed meats, may also be detrimental in our food. For information regarding scientific research and data related to animal products and a plant based-diet, I recommend the following resources:

"Forks Over Knives" presents a *"radical but convincing case that modern diseases can be prevented, halted, and often reversed by leaving animal-based and highly refined foods off the plate ... and adopting a whole-food, plant-based diet instead"* (from www.forksoverknives.com). In this DVD, T. Colin Campbell, PhD and Caldwell Esselstyn, Jr. MD provide valuable insights on a plant based diet based on their scientific and medical research.

Dr. T. Colin Campbell and his son Thomas Campbell II, a physician, document their findings in greater detail in their best seller *The China Study*. This book describes research on consumption of animal products in relationship to chronic illnesses such as coronary heart disease, diabetes, and cancer of the breast, prostate, and bowel. Their conclusion is that people who eat a whole-food, plant based diet with less processed foods and refined carbohydrates will prevent, reduce, or reverse the development of numerous diseases.

Juice Plus (not a vitamin) provides whole food based nutrition from a wide variety of fruits and vegetables. It is backed by more than 25 published clinical studies confirming the health benefits of their products. Sponsoring universities include those in Germany, Italy, Austria, Japan, Australia, and England as well as Vanderbilt University School of Medicine, University of Texas/MD Anderson (cancer hospital), University of California, Wake Forest University, Yale University, and other American institutions. Juice Plus fruits and vegetables are dispensed in capsules or a gummy version, while Juice Plus Complete, a vegan protein, comes in powder form.

Weight Control

An issue that is often discussed in relationship to a plant based diet is that of body weight. Basically, the more sugar we eat, the more insulin is required. Increased amounts of insulin lead to greater fat storing hormone. In other words, your body ends up storing more fat. Read product labels to see how much sugar is in an item. Refined sugars and high fructose syrups should be greatly limited (sodas, candy, cookies, and so on).

Other foods that should be eliminated are white flour, white rice, and white pasta. When possible, reduce or remove processed oils from recipes (some of the recipes in this book do include oil, but, as an alternative, you can use water and steam vegetables). Meat, dairy, and cheese substitutes have fat and sodium. Instead, eat "good fat" items like olive oil, avocados, and nuts.

Stevia, local honey, agave, or 100% maple syrup can be used in place of sugar. For dessert or a snack, we find that our taste buds are well satisfied with the natural sweetness of fruit (a sliced orange at the end of dinner or a handful of grapes during the day). Other options include Chia pudding, ambrosia, or fruit salad. On occasion we enjoy three to four Almond Bites, a delicious little ball of almond ice cream surrounded by rich, flavorful chocolate!

In general, it is best to focus more on fruits and vegetables as well as on "good carbs" like spelt, quinoa, millet, non-wheat noodles, and less on processed foods.

Nutritional Facts

Part of our enjoyment in changing the way we eat is learning nutritional facts. One Thursday night, sitting in front of the fireplace after filling ourselves up with vegan spaghetti, salad, and garlic toast, my friend Martha began to ask questions. I grabbed my computer, totally convinced that Irish potatoes were empty calories! Wow! Was I in for a surprise! They are loaded with vitamin C! That led to exploring other foods to see what was in them. Here are some facts we learned:

1. **Irish Potatoes** have calcium and vitamin C.
2. **Sweet Potatoes** have no fat or cholesterol and minimal sodium BUT, in addition to protein, fiber, and iron, 200g sweet potato is packed with <u>769% Vitamin A</u> and <u>65% Vitamin C!</u>
3. **Cauliflower** (raw) has no fat or cholesterol and minimal sodium, BUT, in addition to protein, fiber, and iron, 100g carries <u>77% Vitamin C</u> and 2% calcium.
4. All **fruits** that we looked up contain protein except lemons!

5. **Nutritional Yeast** has a cheesy flavor and is great on salads, casseroles, soups, and other food. One tablespoon is only 20 calories (no fat); yet it provides <u>100% Thiamin (B1)</u>, <u>160% Riboflavin (B2)</u>, <u>70% Niacin (B3)</u>, <u>140% Pyridoxine (B6)</u>, <u>40% Vitamin B12</u>, <u>40% Folic Acid</u>, <u>30% Pantothenic Acid</u>, 6% Zinc, and 10% Selenium. Note that Vitamin B12 helps with memory and energy levels.
6. **Soy** is a good source of protein. However, there is some controversy about the disadvantages of too much **soy**. True or false? My "take" is to find balance. We use tofu and other soy products, but, to avoid getting too much soy, we blend other protein rich foods such as nuts, quinoa, and beans with a variety of fruits and vegetables.
7. Some folks are allergic to gluten products (products with wheat). There are other options that can be utilized. For instance, instead of flour based noodles, **use rice noodles, quinoa noodles** (a substance historically used by Egyptians because of its high protein quality), and (our favorite and also cheaper) gluten free **corn noodles.**
8. **Shitake mushrooms** are a great way to add a meaty texture to soups, salads, burgers, and casseroles! But did you know that they also boost the immune system with their antioxidants, amino acids, Omega 3 + 6? In fact, one cup of dry Shitake mushrooms (15 g) carries 33% of the recommended daily requirements of iron, 3 g or 12% fiber, and 3% Vitamin C. Shitake mushrooms also provide selenium, copper, potassium, magnesium, and natural enzymes to the diet. Just five ounces of dried Shitake mushrooms provide 27.5% Vitamin B3, 21.3% Vitamin B5, 21% Vitamin B6, 18.2% Vitamin B12, 14.1% Fiber, 7% Vitamin D, 6.3% Protein.

9. **Jicama or Yam Bean** is a fun food that can be eaten raw in salads or cooked in stir fries and casseroles. Either way it has the texture of water chestnuts with a mild apple type flavor. Surprisingly, 1 cup of jicama contains 24% fiber, 1 g protein, and very few calories (46)! It also has 40% Vitamin C and 4% Iron while carrying 0% cholesterol, fat, or sodium.

Conclusion

Dr. Dean Ornish states that 95% of diseases in America are preventable and often reversible through diet and lifestyle changes. Please note that while a plant based diet has been shown to halt diseases like arteriosclerosis or hardening of the arteries, prevent cancer, and eradicate the need for medications such as those prescribed for high blood pressure and diabetes, we do not endorse stopping medication without a doctor's orders.

Substitutions and Tips

Vegan, or plant based, products are becoming so popular that grocery stores now have entire sections for their placement. The following list represents some of the items we have used. Keep in mind that the <u>best</u> choices are not processed foods but whole foods … fresh fruits, vegetables, nuts, and seeds.

Bacon	Lightlife Smart Bacon (Bob sprinkles with garlic powder to enhance its flavor)
Beef	Boca American burgers, Boca meatless crumbles
Butter	Earth Balance (soy free)
Cheese	Daiya cheddar or Daiya Jalapeno (bar or shredded vegan cheeses), homemade cheese (see **Macaroni and Cheese** recipe or check out internet for recipes); Nutritional Yeast (low fat, low sodium, deactivated yeast - not Brewer's yeast - that replaces cheese in some recipes).
Chicken/turkey	Tofurky sliced sandwich meat, seitan (wheat product), Trader Joe's "chicken" strips (there are several other products … we watch for sales and freeze!)
Cream cheese	Tofutti cream cheese
Dressings	Make your own salad dressings (see recipes). May add **Cashew Cream** to thicken (see **"Chicken" Vegetable Soup** recipe)
Eggs	Ener-G Egg Replacer
Hotdogs	Yves Corndogs, Lightlife Smart Dogs
Ice cream	Almond Bites, soy and rice ice creams and ice cream sandwiches
Mayonnaise	Vegenaise

Milk (cow's)	Almond milk (we like vanilla almond milk), Coconut milk, Soy milk
Pasta	Sam Mills gluten free corn noodles, quinoa or rice noodles, or whole wheat noodles
Rice	Royal Rice Blend (white, brown, wild, and red rice) or rice blend in bulk from Whole Foods. We generally prefer quinoa in place of rice as a base for stir fry or in salads. It has a significant amount of protein and the uncooked grain can be kept in sealed jars until ready to cook.
Salt	Mrs. Dash Lemon Pepper (or buy lemon pepper in bulk at Whole Foods), lemon gives the flavor of salt
Sandwiches	Instead of Vegenaise, try one of the following before adding sandwich filling 1. spread bread with hummus (watch for sales and freeze containers of hummus) 2. spread bread with butter substitute (we use Earth Balance) and garlic, then toast 3. spread bread with **Cucumber Dip** (see recipe) 4. spread bread with **Cashew Cream** (see **"Chicken" Vegetable Soup** for recipe) to which 1 tbsp. nutritional yeast, ½ tsp. Dijon mustard, and ½ tsp. lemon juice have been added 5. mash avocado and spread on bread; for extra zing, add 1-2 tbsp. salsa to avocado
Sausage	Boca links, Lightlife Gimme Lean Sausage (see Bob's recipe for **Sausage Patties** using spices purchased at Academy Sports)

Soups	To thicken soups, try one of the following: 1. make a white sauce (as in **Mushroom Soup**) 2. puree half the soup (as in **Broccoli Soup**) 3. make **Cashew Cream** (as in **"Chicken" Vegetable Soup**)
Sour cream	Tofutti sour cream
Spices	Mrs. Dash Original (or purchase herbs/spices in bulk at Whole Foods)
Sugar	stevia, agave, honey
Tomatoes	Metal in cans reportedly leaches and gets into food, staying in our bodies for weeks; replace a 28 ounce can with about four softball size tomatoes. (At season's end, we purchase large amounts of tomatoes on sale, core and freeze them in gallon containers. When ready to use, place frozen tomatoes under warm tap water so skin sloughs off, cook and dice).

Sample Weekly Meal Plan

A weekly meal plan helps organize and take pressure off meal time preparation! Since I was an older parent, home schooling two sons, taking care of elderly parents, AND working a part to full time job, I needed all the help I could get! Planning ahead, even preparing enough to freeze a few meals, has reduced stress and assured that my family gets well balanced meals ... regardless of where my brain is on any given day!

I bypass the weekly meal plan for a monthly calendar of main meals (see back of book for sample, blank copy, and my grocery list). We try to eat a big midday meal, allowing plenty of time for food to digest. Smaller meals in the early evening help prevent insomnia. Eliminate sugar, heavy amounts of vegetables, caffeinated beverages, or salty foods in the evening unless you plan to be awake all night! Meanwhile, fruit contains substances that actually <u>help</u> people sleep better.

Notice that this meal plan portrays a large amount of food! Realistically, I only drink my coffee and a smoothie (loaded with fruits, vegetables, protein, and omegas) for breakfast. Often, my evening meal consists of slices of apple or pear loaded with crunchy peanut butter.

In the meantime, <u>never waste food</u>! We reserve Saturdays as "leftover day" but, if you can't eat it this week, freeze it! Leftovers can also be used in stir fry or added to a freezer container to be used in soups or casseroles!

*Items in **bold** are recipes in this book.*

SUNDAY BREAKFAST:
Granola with orange juice (or soy yogurt!)
Herbal tea with local wildflower honey

Vegan Cuisine

SUNDAY DINNER:
Oriental Stir Fry (add one can black beans)
Assorted fresh fruit (strawberries, apples, grapes)

SUNDAY SUPPER:
Lemon Cumato Sandwiches
Garbanzo Bean Salad

MONDAY BREAKFAST:
Omelet with salsa
Bob's Biscuits
Fresh fruit
Coffee with almond milk and wildflower honey

MONDAY DINNER:
Bob's Sweet and Sour "Chicken"
Broccoli Casserole
Tossed Salad with **Red Wine Vinegar Dressing**
Almond Bites

MONDAY SUPPER:
Amanda's Taco Soup
Cornbread (or **Guacamole** and crackers or sliced vegetables)

TUESDAY BREAKFAST:
Oatmeal with bite size pieces of Vegan Sausage Links (Bob's preference!)
OR Oatmeal with raisins or other fruit, nuts, Earth Balance butter substitute, and brown sugar (Vivian's preference!)
Orange juice mixed with cranberry juice

TUESDAY DINNER:
Stir Fry Spaghetti

Tossed Salad with **Vivian's Ranch Dressing**
Garlic toast
Almond Peach Pie

TUESDAY SUPPER:
Chik-N-Salad
Butternut Succotash
Toast or crackers

WEDNESDAY BREAKFAST:
Bob's Whole Wheat Pancakes topped with sliced fresh fruit
Sausage Patties
Chai tea with almond milk and wildflower honey

WEDNESDAY DINNER:
Meatless Loaf with Sauce
Cauli-Bean Mash
Grilled Vegies
Pumpkin Pie

WEDNESDAY SUPPER:
Stir Fry Burgers
Granny's Favorite Ambrosia

THURSDAY BREAKFAST:
Tomato Quiche (using leftover omelet mix)
Cantaloupe
Vegan Bacon (sprinkle with garlic powder before frying!)

THURSDAY DINNER:
Sausage and Kraut
Mashed Red Potatoes
Broccoli with cheese sauce

Vegan Cuisine

THURSDAY SUPPER:
OLT Sandwiches
Sweet Potato Fries or Tots
Apple slices with peanut butter

FRIDAY BREAKFAST:
Cheese toast (spread vegan cheese on bread, broil to melt)
Soy yogurt with fruit

FRIDAY DINNER:
Macaroni and Cheese
Peas with fresh mushrooms
Pineapple Coleslaw

FRIDAY SUPPER:
Broccoli Soup

APPETIZERS

Chik-N-Salad Dip

*Eating the same thing day after day is no fun. It helps to have a variety of ways to serve a base dish. Left over **Chik-N-Salad** (see recipe) can be frozen or made into this dip.*

Using the ingredients from our **Chik-N-Salad**, place all items in food processor and pulse until blended. This does not have the texture of chicken salad, but it retains the flavor while being smooth enough for dipping with fresh sliced vegetables, crackers, chips, or rice cakes.

(Optional) Add 2 tablespoons Hickory Barbeque Sauce to 1 cup of Chik-N-Salad dip.

Cream Cheese Celery Stuffing

In 1979, Mother lost a four year battle to cancer. During her illness, she suggested that, after her death, Dad and her best friend marry! Neither Dad nor Mavis thought much of her plan. However, within a year they wed, and Mavis became one of my dearest friends. She nurtured my relationship with Daddy, listened to my joys and concerns, and humbly prayed for me along with her own children. Daddy would attest to the fact that, not only had he married a wonderful, loving woman, but he'd also married another great cook! Here's my version of her stuffed celery.

8 oz. Tofutti cream cheese
½ cup diced olives (green or black)
Onion juice (grate ½ onion)
½ cup pecans or walnuts (chopped)

2 Tbsp. Vegenaise
(Optional) crushed pecans or walnuts

Pulse together in food processor. Add juice from the can of olives for extra moisture and flavor. Stuff into two inch slices of celery sticks.

Cucumber Dip

2 medium large cucumbers (peel, remove seeds)
8 oz. Tofutti cream cheese
2 cloves fresh garlic, minced
4 Tbsp. fresh chopped chives (stems of green onions)
3 Tbsp. dill, chopped
2 tsp. black pepper

Place cucumbers in food processor and pulse. Add remaining ingredients. Refrigerate overnight so flavors are more enhanced. Use as a dip with wheat thins or vegetables.

Fruit and Nut Energy Bars

As a hospice nurse, I often saw six to nine patients in a day. Instead of taking a long lunch break, I enjoyed going outside with an energy bar and drink to finish my paperwork. This energy bar is a quick pick-me-up that lasts until dinner.

1 cup dates
½ cup raisins

½ cup cherry flavored cranberries
1 cup assortment of nuts (such as almonds, pecans, walnuts)
2 teaspoons almond extract
¼ cup water

Place all ingredients in food processor for several minutes until blended. Press into medium size muffin tins. Freeze overnight; then carefully pry out of tins with dull knife and store in bag or container in freezer.

Guacamole

I was blessed with a mom who taught me how to manage a home, cook, stretch a dollar, and more. Growing up sixty miles southeast of Houston, Texas, I quickly learned to love her Mexican dishes. Here is a quick and easy version of Mother's guacamole.

1 ripe avocado (soft to a little nutty)
½ cup salsa (we use mild)
2 tsp. Worcestershire sauce
1 tsp. garlic powder
2 tsp. lemon juice

Mash avocado with a fork, add remaining ingredients and stir. This is great with chips or crackers but is also delicious as a dip with diced or sliced carrots, green peppers, broccoli, cucumbers, and cauliflower.

Pepperoni Dip

After Mother's death, Dad married Mavis. She often encouraged us to go places without her (so we could have time together!) Daddy would tell Mavis how proud he was of me .... and she would tell me! I loved her for that, for being his voice to me. She gave me my father's blessing, something he never got from his own parents. She also gave me some delicious recipes that I "veganized!"

½ package vegan pepperoni or diced lunch meat (like Tofurky)
¼ bell pepper, chopped
1 cups Vegenaise (or **Vivian's Ranch Dressing**)
1 8-ounce tubs Tofutti cream cheese
Blenderize ingredients and serve with chips.

Spinach Dip

This dip is loaded with spinach as well as flavor! No one will ever know it's vegan!

1 cup Vegenaise
14 oz. container Tofutti sour cream
1 pkg. Knorr vegetable recipe mix
16 oz. pkg. frozen, chopped spinach
(optional) 1 can water chestnuts (chopped)

Cook spinach, cool, and squeeze out liquids. Mix ingredients together and serve with vegetables or crackers. While this is delicious right away, the flavor permeates the dip and tastes much better the next day.

BEVERAGES

Bob's Thirst Quenching Tea

2 Green tea bags (we use decaffeinated)
8 cups water
1 cup stevia
1/2 cup lemon juice (bottled)
8 cups cold water
(Optional) 2 squeezed lemons instead of bottled lemon juice
(Optional) Handful of mint leaves

Boil 2 tea bags in 8 cups water. Let steep an hour or longer. Add stevia and stir until dissolved. Add lemon juice or entire lemons with squeezed juice plus 8 cups cold water. Stir and store in refrigerator.

Coconut Pineapple Smoothie

We always have bananas and frozen strawberries on hand. If a banana begins to turn brown, I freeze it. Warm water over a frozen banana causes the skin to loosen and peel off. Meanwhile, frozen fruit makes a thicker smoothie!

1 cup pineapple juice (or 1 can crushed pineapple with juice)
2 cups coconut milk
1 banana (preferably frozen ahead of time but may be fresh)
7-10 medium to large frozen strawberries
1/2 cup agave syrup, honey, or stevia

Chop and mix in blender. Partially slice a strawberry and put on rim of stemmed glass, serve smoothie with a straw!

Fruit Tea

2 Green tea bags
8 cups water
1 cup Stevia
4 cups cold water
2 cups orange juice
½ cup lemon juice (may use lemonade)
2 cups cranberry juice

Boil 2 tea bags in 8 cups water. Let steep an hour or two. Add stevia and stir until dissolved. Split liquid into two gallon size containers. Add orange juice, lemon juice, and cranberry juice and additional water. Stir and store in refrigerator.

Hot Spiced Tea

I love a cup of hot tea during the winter, but it also makes great birthday, Christmas, or teachers' gifts. Mix a large batch and freeze in smaller bags or containers so that it stays fresh and is available for a gift that says "I care"!

4 cups instant (powdered) orange juice
2 cups instant tea (may use decaffeinated)
3 cups instant (powdered, sugar already added) lemonade
6 cups sugar (or Stevia, but may need more than 6 cups)
2 tsp. cloves
2 tsp. cinnamon
2 tsp. nutmeg

Mix ingredients together. Use 2 to 3 Tablespoons mixture per cup of hot water.

Nanoberry Smoothies

Many years ago I learned about Juice Plus capsules packed with a variety of organic dehydrated fruits and vegetables. Later a nurse coworker told me about Nano Greens (vegetables), Nano Reds (fruit), Nano Omegas, and Nano Pros (protein). Nanos come in powder form and can be added to water, juice, or milk. I call these our daily "power drinks" because, even before we changed to a plant-based diet, they significantly reduced illness in our home.

2 bananas
7-10 large frozen strawberries
3 scoops Nano Greens
1 scoop each Nano Reds and Nano Omegas
½ to 1 scoop Juice Plus Complete (this is vegan while Nano Pro contains whey)
2 cups Cranberry Juice (may use vanilla almond milk)

Place bananas in blender, add strawberries (if frozen items dropped in first, they get stuck in blades of blender). Then add remaining ingredients and blend for 15 seconds. Makes 3 large smoothies. *(See Suggested Resources for product information).*

BREADS & CEREALS

Bob's Biscuits

Bob loves homemade biscuits. I do, too, when he makes my favorite breakfast of Fried Green Tomatoes, biscuits, and gravy! Biscuits are also delicious with wildflower honey!

2 cups whole wheat flour
4 tsp. baking powder
½ tsp. cream of tarter
½ tsp. salt
3 tsp. stevia
5 Tbsp. Earth Balance butter substitute
2/3-1 cup vanilla almond milk

Mix flour, baking powder, cream of tartar, salt, and stevia. Cut butter substitute into flour mixture. Slowly add milk while blending ingredients together. Roll out dough (1 inch thick) and cut into circles using 2 inch biscuit cutter or glass. Bake in 450 degree oven for 10-12 minutes until biscuits brown.

Fried Green Tomatoes

1-2 green tomatoes
2/3 cup whole wheat flour
3 Tbsp. butter substitute
2/3-1 cup vanilla almond milk
Lemon pepper

Slice tomatoes and coat with whole wheat flour. Fry in small amount of oil until lightly browned on each side. Remove tomatoes from pan and set aside. Melt butter substitute in pan with drippings from tomatoes. Blend in leftover whole wheat flour (at least 2 Tbsp.), seasoning, and then milk, cooking on medium heat until thickens into gravy. Serve tomatoes and gravy over biscuits!

Bob's Whole Wheat Pancakes

TRADITION! When Nick and Ryan were young, Bob made pancakes on Saturday mornings! This revised version is so tasty you can eat them without butter or syrup OR you can smother a stack of pancakes with an assortment of fresh fruit!

2½ cups whole wheat flour
2 Tbsp. baking powder
3 Tbsp. stevia
1 tsp. salt
2 Tbsp. Ener-G Egg Replacer
2 cups vanilla almond milk
4 Tbsp. canola oil

Mix dry ingredients. Stir in milk and oil. If batter is too thick, add more milk until fairly runny. Pour batter into greased nonstick skillet (in 6-8 inch circles). Bake on medium heat (high heat tends to burn) until bubbles open up on top of each pancake. Flip pancakes, and bake 1 more minute.

Cornbread

1 c. whole wheat flour
1 c corn meal (may also add corn kernels and 1-2 Tb. Taco seasoning)
¼ c. sugar (can use stevia)
¾ tsp. salt
4 tsp. baking powder (aluminum free)
4 Tbsp. Ener-G Egg Replacer
¼ c. safflower oil
1 ½ c. vanilla almond milk

Mix dry ingredients together. Then add liquids. If consistency is too dry, add more almond milk. Place mix in a greased pan (12 inch cast iron skillet or 8X8 baking dish) or muffin tins. Bake 20 to 25 minutes at 425 degrees. Serve cornbread with a skillet of stir fry, bowl of soup, or mess of beans and rice with fresh onions chopped up and served on top!

Granola

We purchase honey from local distributors (which is supposed to be good for your immune system). We prefer the rich bodied flavor of wildflower honey, a delicious addition to tea, coffee, and recipes such as this Granola (our sons Nick and Ryan like orange juice on their cereal instead of milk!)

4 cups oats
2 cups wheat flakes
1 cup bran
1 cup wheat germ

Vivian Cate

¾ cups raisins
¾ cups dried cranberries (cherry flavored)
1 cup walnuts or pecans
½ cup chia seeds
½ cup sunflower seeds
(optional) 1 cup coconut
2-3 tsp. cinnamon
2 tsp. nutmeg
½ cup oil
1 cup wildflower honey (from local distributor)

Warm oil and honey. Mix remaining ingredients and blend in warm liquids. Bake on cookie sheet for 20 to 30 minutes at 250 degrees. Store in sealed jars or freeze.

Joanie's Dressing

The Thanksgiving before Mother died of breast cancer, she had me place a TV tray in front of her couch so she could help prepare the family meal! I am so grateful that I wrote down those recipes! My favorite is her dressing, moist and unlike any I've ever tasted. Serve with Whole Foods vegan turkey or as a side dish with vegetables (stuffing mix may have milk or egg products).

3 pkg. herb stuffing mix
2 recipes prepared cornbread (or 13X9 pan)
4 tsp. Ener-G Egg Replacer
2 large onions (chopped)
1 while bunch of celery (diced)
Sage, lemon pepper (we like a LOT!)
4 apples (peeled and diced)

Pecans or walnuts (about 1 cup)
Fresh mushrooms (8 oz. chopped)

Crumble cornbread and add rest of ingredients. Add enough almond milk (about 3-4 cups) to moisten mixture. Cover and bake in pans (use four 8X8 or two 13X9 baking dishes) for about 1-1 ½ hours at 350 degrees. This freezes well.

Momma's Christmas Sweet Rolls

I love traditions! When my brother Scott and I were young, Momma would make these sweet rolls on Christmas morning! MMMMM good! And oh so easy to make!

½ cup melted butter substitute
½ cup brown sugar
½ cup finely chopped walnuts or pecans
10 ounce container candied fruit
1 recipe of biscuits (or a can of 8-10 medium sized biscuits)

Melt butter substitute in a glass 8X8 cake dish at 350 degrees. Stir in brown sugar and smooth. Sprinkle nuts and spread candied fruit (just like making pineapple upside down cake). Then set uncooked biscuits side-by-side on top. Bake at 350 for 10 to 15 minutes or until biscuits brown. Immediately turn over onto large serving platter or it sticks to pan. These can be frozen ahead of time and warmed.

Sweet Potato Muffins

I found this recipe many years ago when babysitting for a friend. Since 200 g of sweet potatoes pack a whopping 769% Vitamin A, 65% Vitamin C, plus protein, fiber, and iron, this makes a healthy snack as well as a tasty addition to the meal!

1 ½ cup whole wheat flour
½ cup sugar or honey
2 tsp. baking powder
1 or more tsp. each of cinnamon and nutmeg
½ cup almond milk
½ cup (1 small to medium) mashed cooked sweet potato
½ cup melted Earth Balance butter substitute
2 Tbsp. Ener-G Egg Replacer
¾ cup chopped walnuts or pecans

Mix all ingredients, fill muffin tins (about 2/3 full), and bake for 18 to 20 minutes at 400 degrees.

DESSERTS

Almond Peach Pie

Our freezer was FULL of dried peaches! I had purchased them from a homeschool mom whose family was adopting a special needs child from another country. They needed funds for the adoption and medical expenses. Since our guys are adopted, I have a heart for helping other families …. maybe to an extreme in this case! I bought eleven buckets (5 gallons each) of dried peaches! I gave away as much as friends would gracefully take. I made chutney and even tried several cobbler recipes. This pie finally won our praise!

¾ c stevia or sugar
5 cups dehydrated peaches (may use fresh or canned peaches)
2-3 tsp. cinnamon
1 Tbsp. almond extract
4 Tbsp. whole wheat flour
2 deep dish pie crusts
4-5 Tbsp. Earth Balance butter substitute

Cook dehydrated peaches in water until tender. Dice into 1" pieces. Mix first five ingredients together and pour into first pie crust. Dot with butter substitute and cover with second pie crust. Using a fork, mash edges together and trim off remaining dough. Poke fork into top crust 4-5 times. Then bake pie in 350 degree oven for 35 minutes. Serve as is or top with almond milk ice cream (or may pour ¼ to ½ cup almond milk over hot pie or cover with a slice of vegan cheddar cheese).

Vivian Cate

Annie Lucenia's Apple Pie

Bob's dad was one of fourteen children! Annie Harrison Armistead married James Henry Cate in November of 1887 and had five children. When Grandma died in 1896, her little sister, Mary Lucenia Armistead, helped care for the children. A few years later, she and Granddaddy married and had nine more children! While Annie Lucenia was only seven years younger than Bob's Dad Wilbur, she was actually his niece and daughter of the first of those fourteen children! I adored Aunt Cenie (as I called her) and have this pie to remind me of her joy and love!

4 cups apples, cut into eighths
1 cup sugar
1 cup orange juice
1 cup Earth Balance butter substitute

Cook ingredients until it begins to clear. Meanwhile, prepare your favorite pie crust dough. For a flavorful crust, add orange juice instead of water to flour and butter substitute. Gently pour apple mixture into pie crust and place lattice on top.

For those who purchase pie crusts, use the first crust as your foundation, add apple mixture, and lay the second crust on top. Press the edges together with a fork and cut off excess crust. Poke a fork into the top four or five times for ventilation.

Bake at 450 degrees for 10 minutes. Then turn to 350 degrees for 30 minutes.

Chia Pudding

A hospice nurse introduced me to Chai <u>tea</u>. Several years later, we learned that Chia <u>seeds</u> are a wonderful thickener for puddings and pies. Nutritionally, Chia enhances digestion, lowers cholesterol and stabilizes blood sugar. It also has significant amounts of fiber, omega-3 fats, calcium, phosphorus, and manganese. As if that's not enough, try this delicious dessert at the end of a heavy meal! Be sure to experiment with other seasonal fruits!

1 3/4 cups vanilla almond milk
½ cup Chia seed
3 Tbsp. stevia (or sugar)
3 Tbsp. maple syrup
1 tsp. vanilla extract
7-10 large strawberries
1 banana

Mix ingredients together in a food processor (or blender) and pour into bowls or glasses. Top with a strawberry and refrigerate for one to two hours to allow pudding to thicken.

Chia Banana Pudding

Omit strawberries from **Chia Pudding** recipe. Add 2 bananas to remaining ingredients and pulse in food processor. Line a square Pyrex dish with 2 additional bananas (sliced) and pour mixture on top. Cover with vanilla wafers. (Since wafers can become soggy, place them on top of pudding instead of underneath!)

Chia Pie

Mix ingredients for **Chia Pudding** together in a food processor and pour into a graham cracker pie crust. Sprinkle crushed nuts on top. Freeze for one to two hours. Remove frozen pies 30" prior to serving.

Key Lime Chia Pie

½ cup vanilla almond milk
12 ounce can frozen limeade concentrate
½ cup Chia seed
4 Tbsp. stevia (or sugar)
3 Tbsp. maple syrup
1 graham cracker pie crust

Mix first five ingredients together in blender. Pour into a bowl and store in freezer for one to two hours (ingredients will be very thin at first). Remove bowl and pour ingredients into pie crust. Place back in freezer over night or until thickened.

Ice Cream

When in my early 20s, a friend and I would eat an entire half gallon of ice cream in one sitting. Not helpful for the waste-line, but it sure was good! Vegan ice cream is just as tempting! I blended recipes to make this delicious and easy ice cream in our electric ice cream freezer!

2 cups So Delicious Vanilla Coconut Creamer
3 cups vanilla almond milk
½ cup sugar
Pinch of salt
Bag of crushed ice
Box of ice cream salt
Electric freezer

Mix together creamer, milk, sugar, and salt until sugar dissolves. Pour into ice cream freezer and surround with crushed ice and ice cream salt as per directions on freezer. Plug in and let it churn for about 30 minutes until motor begins to slow down. Ice cream will be soft but, IF you don't eat it all first, can go into the freezer to harden!

Pumpkin Pie

One Christmas, we noticed huge orange balls (pumpkins) floating down the creek that runs behind our home. The next year, Bob asked neighbors if we could have those leftover porch decorations! Bob experimented until the following recipe was developed! We like ours spicy!

3 deep dish pie crusts
5 cups fresh pureed pumpkin (cook chunks of pumpkin, puree in food processor)
1 ½ c. So Delicious Vanilla Coconut Milk Creamer
½ c. brown sugar
½ c. white stevia
½ tsp. salt
3 Tbsp. Ener-G Egg Replacer
1 Tbsp. cinnamon

Vivian Cate

1 tsp. ginger
½ tsp. each nutmeg, cloves (optional: ¼ tsp. allspice)

Partially cook pie crusts for 10" at 425 degrees. Blend 3 cups pureed pumpkin with remaining ingredients. Pour into partially cooked pie crusts and bake at 400 degrees for 45 minutes or until knife, inserted about 1/3 way from edge of pie, comes out clean.

Note: A pumpkin about the size of a basketball should yield close to 10 cups of pureed pumpkin for 6 pies.

Ryan's Pineapple Upside Down Cake

This is one of Ryan's specialties. In fact, he made this cake for Aunt Martha's father's 100th birthday! The secret ingredient (almond extract) makes this a cake folks will ask for over and over again!

1 box white or yellow cake mix
3 Tbsp. Ener-G Egg Replacer
½ c. Earth Balance butter substitute (melted)
1 ¼ c. water
2 tsp. almond extract
4 Tbsp. Earth Balance butter substitute (melted)
1/3 c. brown sugar
20 oz. can sliced pineapples (drained)
8oz. jar maraschino cherries

Set oven to 350 degrees. Blend together first five ingredients. Set aside. Melt 4 Tbsp. butter substitute with brown sugar in a 9X13 inch cake dish (do this in the oven). Place slices of pineapple across bottom of cake dish (on top of melted butter/ sugar). Put cherries in center of each sliced pineapple and pour batter over fruit. Bake 30 to 35 minutes. Slightly cool; then turn cake over onto large platter.

Strawberry Rhubarb Pie

One day at the grocery store I saw a couple waiting for assistance with rhubarb. Curiosity got the best of me, and I asked what they did with this plant that looks a bit like overgrown celery. The husband began to tell me that his wife makes THE best pies around! Rhubarb is rather expensive, so I add fresh strawberries for a mouth-watering pie that freezes well for company!

3 stalks rhubarb, cut in 1 inch slices
1 cups strawberries, quartered
1 cup sugar
3 Tbsp. whole wheat flour
1-2 tsp. zest of orange peel (grated skin)
2 Tbsp. butter substitute
2 pie crusts

Combine all ingredients and let stand 5 minutes. Pour into first pie crust and dot with butter substitute. Cover with second pie crust and pinch edges together. Using a fork, punch 4-5 sets of holes in top crust. Bake at 400 degrees for 50 minutes.

NOTE: I often triple the recipe, baking 3 pies at a time. Cover two cooled pies completely with saran wrap and freeze for later!

ENTREES

Barbecue "Chicken"

Growing up in Texas, we ate a LOT of barbeque! Here's our vegan alternative!

1 large onion (sliced into strips)
½ to 2/3 cup barbeque sauce (we like hickory smoked)
1 box or bag of chicken substitute (strips or cutlets)

Sauté onion slices in a water or tablespoon oil. Add barbeque sauce and stir. Place cutlets in pan and spoon sauce over top. Cover and simmer 10 minutes. Turn cutlets, moving sauce and onions to top of cutlets. Remove from heat but leave lid on for another few minutes before serving.

Black-eyed Pea Veggie Casserole

Sometimes, I purchase ingredients seen on a package in the grocery store, go home, and recreate the meal! Such is the case with this hearty casserole. It freezes well plus black eyed peas are a very good source of protein, iron, and fiber!

1 cup rice (brown, wild, red rice blend)
1 pkg. black eyed peas (frozen or precooked)
Water

Assorted fresh or frozen vegetables such as broccoli, mushrooms, grated carrots, onions, corn, red pepper, water chestnuts (can use Stir Fry mix from Costco)

1-2 tsp. Mrs. Dash seasoning or spices to taste
2 Tbsp. Earth Balance
(Optional) Soy sauce to taste

Cook rice in two cups water until tender. Steam black eyed peas and other vegetables. Blend all ingredients together and serve with cornbread.

Bob's Sweet and Sour Chicken

10 oz. jar of sweet & sour Sauce (we use Kroger brand)
20 oz. can crushed pineapple (drained thoroughly)
(optional) 1 tsp. horseradish

Mix ingredients, place in lidded containers. Serve over cooked "chicken" patties.

Bumble Bean Stew

Add leftover meat substitutes, vegetables, rice, quinoa, or fruit to a sealed gallon bag or container in the freezer. When full, use the mixture in soup, stir fry, pot pie, or casseroles!

2 cups **Mixed Dried Beans** (see following recipe)
1 package mixed frozen vegetables (or 2 cups leftover mixture)
1 large can diced tomatoes (or 4 medium to large diced fresh tomatoes)
1 large onion, chopped
1-2 cloves garlic, minced

2 tsp. each Mrs. Dash original seasoning and Mrs. Dash lemon pepper

Soak beans in hot water for an hour. Drain. Pour into crockpot, fill with water, and cook on low for 6 to 8 hours. Sautee onion and garlic. Add remaining ingredients to beans. Cook on high until vegetables are tender. Serve with cornbread!

Mixed Dried Beans

16 ounce package dried split peas
16 ounce package dried red or yellow lentils
16 ounces package dried kidney or black beans or black-eyed peas
16 ounce package dried northern, chick pea, or garbanzo beans

Mix beans together. Pour into 2 cup sealed containers. Freeze until ready to use.

Chik-N-Salad

I used to love chicken salad. When I started seeing chickpea (or garbanzo bean) salad recipes, I experimented and came up with the following recipe. It makes a great stuffed tomato entrée or **Chik-N-Salad sandwich.** *Try each of the following options for change in flavor. We like all of them!*

1 can garbanzo beans (chickpea)
1 can white northern beans
1 cup steamed quinoa (1/2 cup quinoa in 1 cup water)

Vivian Cate

½ medium diced onion
½ cup sliced celery
¾ cup shredded carrots
1 diced green pepper
¾ cup diced bread and butter pickles
    OR dill pickles (depending on flavor desired)
1 cup chopped walnuts
¼ cup sunflower seeds
2 teaspoons Mrs. Dash
    OR 2 teaspoons curry powder (depending on flavor desired)
Grapes (Optional but especially good with curry)
¾-1 cup Vegenaise

Place beans and Vegenaise in food processor. Pulse until smooth. Add to remaining ingredients and mix together. Serve in bed of lettuce with tomato wedges. Makes a meal by itself but can also be served with fresh fruit and choice of muffins or garlic toast.

Chili

Chili is so delicious on a cold winter day! My favorite way to eat chili is on a bed of corn chips and covered with melted cheese!

1 can kidney beans
1 can northern beans
(Optional) 1 package ground meatless crumbles
1 large can tomatoes (or 4 large tomatoes, diced)
1 package of Chili powder (or Chili seasoning to taste)

Mix ingredients and simmer until warm. Serve over corn chips with vegan cheese on top. This freezes well.

Vegan Cuisine

Chili Enchiladas

Every Thanksgiving our family used to drive eight hours to Matamoros, Mexico where we did our Christmas shopping and ate the "real deal." Now I live far from the border, so I improvise!

Drain off most of the liquid from **Chili** (save liquid for soup!) Place several tablespoons of drained **Chili** down the center of a tortilla, fold sides around chili and place seam down in 9X13 dish (or divide into two 8X8 dishes and freeze one dish). Cover with grated Daiya cheese (cheddar or jalapeno), and bake in 350 degree oven for 20-30 minutes until warm. Serve as is or with salsa, sour cream, avocado or guacamole, and a side of rice.

Delicious Pot Pies

My maternal grandfather, Papa Peter Graeff, did not speak English until he was 21 years old. He and Grandma Ossie Baugher on my father's side were of Pennsylvania Dutch (German) descent. Several Amish and Mennonite recipes were passed down, but pot pies are a favorite. We like ours thick with vegetables, just enough sauce to blend everything together. Pot pies freeze well so make two or three!

Option #1: Bumble Bean Pot Pie

Drain most of liquid from **Bumble Bean Stew** (save liquid for soup), pour into pie crust. Top with 4 or 5 teaspoons butter substitute, cover with second pie crust and seal edges with fork. Poke 4 to 5 sets of holes in top with fork for ventilation, and bake in a 350 degree oven until crust is brown (about 45 minutes).

Option #2: Chili Pot Pie or Taco Pot Pie

Drain excess liquid from **Chili** or from **Taco Soup** (see recipes) and pour into pie crust. Continue as instructed in Option #1.

Option #3: Vegetable Pot Pie

Cook assorted vegetables (may use leftover stir fry) or frozen mixed vegetables. Add one cup **Mushroom Soup** (see recipe), sautéed onions, mushrooms, and other vegetables. For added protein, add a can of black beans. Pour into pie crust and continue as instructed in Option #1.

Option #4: "Chicken" Pot Pie

Add seitan chunks or imitation "Chicken strips" to cooked mixed vegetables or vegetable stew and 1 cup mushroom soup. Add seasoning such as Mrs. Dash original or sage, lemon pepper, and garlic. Pour into pie crust and continue as instructed in Option #1.

Option #5: "Beef" Pot Pie

Add vegan imitation beef to cooked vegetables with 1 cup mushroom soup. Add seasoning such as Mrs. Dash original. Pour into pie crust and continue as instructed in Option #1.

Vegan Cuisine

Eggplant Spaghetti

Martha comes for dinner once a week, and I take her "Sunday Samplers" when I go to her house on Sundays. This dish was inspired by Martha's daughter!

1 diced eggplant
4 oz. fresh mushrooms (chopped) or 1 cup dried shiitake mushrooms
1 onion (chopped)
1 green pepper (diced)
2-3 cloves fresh garlic (mashed in garlic press)
1 can/jar spaghetti sauce
Garlic powder, oregano, and basil (add to taste)
Spaghetti noodles (cooked; we prefer corn noodles but for additional protein, try quinoa noodles)

Sautee first 5 ingredients in safflower oil (it's best to start with eggplant, onions, and green pepper and add mushrooms last). Add spaghetti sauce and extra spices and heat. Serve over noodles.

Freezer Friendly Family Favorite Fagioli

Before we married, I stopped by a store to get some things for dinner. A little old lady was wandering through the produce department asking people if they wanted a freezer! I got her information and, upon arrival at Bob's house, learned that the lady's husband had worked on the farm where Bob and his daughter Amanda lived. We purchased her little freezer for $25, had it repaired for $40, and received a wedding gift that same day, covering the cost! Freezers are huge money savers!

1 large onion (chopped)
1 cup carrots (shredded in food processor)
2-3 stalks celery (chopped)
2-4 cloves garlic (minced)
1-2 pkg. vegan meat crumbles
2 14.5 oz. cans diced tomatoes
1 15oz.can light red kidney beans or black beans
1 15oz. can northern beans or chick pea beans
1 15oz. can tomato sauce
1 12oz. can tomato juice
2 Tbsp. Worcestershire sauce
1 Tbsp. red wine vinegar
Pepper, basil, oregano, thyme to taste (about ½ to 1 tsp. each)
½ lb. Pasta, cooked

Sautee onion, carrots, celery, and garlic. Add remaining ingredients and simmer until carrots are soft. Add pasta and simmer 10 minutes longer. Makes 3 meals for family of 4 so freeze 2 containers!

Italian Sausage Casserole

1 cup brown rice (cook in 2 ½ cups water)
1 package (4 large links) Tofurky Italian Sausage
1 large onion, diced
2 cloves garlic, minced
1 large green pepper, cut into bite-size pieces
8 ounces mushroom, sliced
2 Tbsp. oil
2 stalks celery, sliced
1 14-ounce can diced tomatoes (with juice)

1 can diced pineapples (save juice)
½ tsp. garlic powder
1 tsp. lemon pepper
4-6 Tbsp. brown sugar
2 Tbsp. corn starch

Cook rice until water absorbed and rice softened. Cut sausage in bite-size slices. Sautee onion, garlic, green pepper, and mushrooms in oil. Drain pineapple juice into pan and add corn starch. Cover and simmer 5 minutes. Mix remaining ingredients with sautéed vegetables and thickened pineapple juice and simmer 3 to 4 minutes.

Lentil Chili

Too many tomatoes in the garden? Cut out stems and bad spots, place in one gallon containers or bags, and freeze. Add to the container until you have collected a gallon of tomatoes. When ready to use them in spaghetti sauce, soup, or this recipe, place each frozen tomato under warm tap water. Skins slough right off! Many years ago, I taped a TV show with this hint. I was told to tap a tomato on the counter, showing that it was frozen. I did, but it slipped out of my hand, hitting the cameraman! So much for a TV career!

2 Lipton "Recipe Secrets" Vegetable soup packets
8 cups water
1 bell pepper, chopped
1 onion, chopped
8 ounces fresh mushrooms, sliced
5 cloves garlic, minced
1 16-ounce package dried lentils (about 2 ½ cups lentils)

Vivian Cate

2 cups diced tomatoes (or one 28 ounce can)
10 ounce can Ro-Tel Mexican diced tomatoes with lemon and cilantro
1 package frozen diced carrots
4 to 5 tsp. chili powder

Sautee onion, bell peppers, mushrooms, and garlic. Add remaining ingredients and bring to boil. Cover and lower heat to simmer for 30 minutes. Remove lid and cook another 10 minutes. Serve with **Bob's Cornbread** or crackers. This freezes well so put half in containers for future meals!

Macaroni and Cheese

<u>Option #1: Traditional Macaroni and Cheese</u>

This method is quick and easy to prepare! Be sure to try different flavored cheeses to find the one you like best. Jalapeno, mozzarella, cheddar, and others are available.

¼ c vegan butter
1-2 Tbsp whole wheat flour
½ cup almond milk
1 pkg Daiya cheese
Mrs. Dash, lemon pepper, and garlic to taste
Macaroni (Sam Mills Corn Pasta)

Melt butter; stir in flour and seasoning. Slowly add milk, stirring while mixture cooks. When thickened, add Daiya cheese or other vegan cheese substitute. Simmer until cheese melts. Meanwhile, cook pasta. Blend cheese mixture into warm, drained noodles, and serve. This can be frozen!

<u>Option #1: Barbeque Macaroni and Cheese</u>

Bob searched online for vegan cheese recipes. Though many included cashews, we settled on an almond version. When I returned to the store to get more nuts, I found <u>barbeque</u> almonds on sale for less than half price and purchased 8 bags. I planned to wash off the seasoning ... until I made a batch of cheese <u>with</u> the seasoning. It is so delicious that it's great as a dip or in the following dish!

3-5 cups water
4 Tbsp. agar powder (or 10 Tbsp. agar flakes; powder is stronger than flakes)
4 Tbsp. coconut oil
3 cup blanched, slivered smoked almonds (or use unseasoned almonds)
2 cups nutritional yeast
1/2 cup white miso
4 Tbsp. tomato paste
2 lemons (juice)
2 Tbsp. onion powder
2 tsp. salt

Mix agar powder and 3 cups water and set aside for a five minutes. Slowly bring agar mixture to boil, adding the coconut oil and stirring occasionally. Turn heat to medium and boil for 3 to 5 minutes until consistency of thick syrup or gelatin.

In the meantime, blend the almonds in food processor until it changes from a mealy consistency to paste. Add miso and nutritional yeast and continue to process until mixture no longer clings to side of container. Add tomato paste, lemon juice, onion powder, and salt and blend thoroughly.

Pour hot agar/coconut oil mixture into food processor and pulse until the consistency of cake batter or cheese sauce. If mixture is too thick, add up to 3 more cups of water and continue to blend.

Move cheese into two rectangular containers or loaf pans and cool uncovered in the refrigerator for 3 hours or overnight. Set aside 1 cup of cheese and freeze remaining cheese in 1 cup chunks.

Grate 1 cup of cheese and stir into hot macaroni. Microwave and stir until creamy texture obtained.

Meatless Loaf with Sauce

Our family loved my meatloaf. This vegan meatloaf resembles our original dish.

8-10 ounces fresh mushrooms
1 medium onion
2 cloves garlic
3 stalks celery
2 pkg. vegetarian meat crumbles (or 1 pkg. crumbles with 1 container firm tofu)
1 ½ cups uncooked oatmeal (or 3/4 cup crushed club crackers & 3/4 cup oats)
1 cup pecans (or walnuts)
2 pkg onion soup mix

2 tablespoons Bragg soy sauce
½ cup catsup
1 Tbsp. Dijon mustard

Add ingredients together. It will be crumbly but press into bread shaped loaves. Preheat oven, bake 45 to 60 minutes at 350 degrees (loaf will be soft inside so may want to microwave 1-2 minutes). Top with sauce. Make several loaves and freeze.

Sweet and Sour Sauce

½ c. chopped onion
½ c. sugar or stevia
½ c. catsup
¼ c. vinegar
2 tsp. Worcestershire sauce

Sautee onion. Mix ingredients, cover and cook for 5 minutes, starting on high and decreasing to simmer.

Omelet

Try this for a breakfast that will fill you up with a smile!

12-14 ounce tub firm tofu, drained
2 Tbsp. almond milk
2 Tbsp. nutritional yeast
4 Tbsp. Ener-G Egg Replacer
1 Tbsp. wheat gluten (we use Bob's Red Mill)

¼ tsp. turmeric
3 Tbsp. stevia (or sugar)
Grated vegan cheese (Daiya)
(Optional mushrooms, onion, green pepper

Blend ingredients in food processor. Place mixture in lightly oiled pan and cook on medium heat. When you can lift it with a spatula, turn and cook the other side OR place sautéed mushrooms, onions, green peppers, and cheese down center of omelet. Close right half over left half and cook about 2 minutes. Then turn to other side and cook another 2 minutes. Serve with Bob's Whole Wheat Biscuits, a side of Boca sausage links, and a glass of juice.

Quesadillas

1 green pepper (chopped)
½ cup red onion (chopped)
½ c. corn (frozen or fresh)
Seitan (a whole wheat chicken-like product) OR other meatless chicken
Pkg. of 8 inch wheat tortillas
6 oz. nondairy cheddar cheese (we use Daiya)

Sautee peppers and onion in a tablespoon of oil. Stir in corn and seitan. Place 4 tortillas on a cutting board, spread each with ¼ of mix plus ¼ cheese. Top with remaining 4 tortillas, press down, and cook (one at a time) in a hot skillet about 2 minutes per side. May top with vegan sour cream, guacamole, and/or salsa.

Vegan Cuisine

Tomato Quiche

I used to say that when I go to Heaven, I'm taking my <u>More with Less</u> cookbook! The recipes are easy and delicious. Better yet, the authors taught me how to use leftovers! Try this delicious quiche, inspired by a recipe from that book!

12-14 ounce tub firm tofu, drained
2 Tbsp. almond milk
2 Tbsp. nutritional yeast
4 Tbsp. Ener-G Egg Replacer
1 Tbsp. vital wheat gluten
¼ tsp. turmeric
2 Tbsp. basil
3 Tbsp. stevia (or sugar)
8 ounces Daiya cheese (Havarti style jalapeño)
2 medium tomatoes (cut into bite size pieces) or 4 large Roma tomatoes
½ large onion
1 Tbsp. basil
2 regular pie crusts (not deep dish)

Preheat oven to 350 degrees. Precook pie crusts for 5 minutes before filling. Process first eight (8) ingredients in food processor. Melt cheese in microwave for 1 minute and stir. Mix processed ingredients with tomatoes, onion, basil, and melted cheese. Pour into pie crusts and bake for 45 minutes. Freeze one pie and serve the other with **Granny's Favorite Ambrosia**. This quiche is also good cold!

Vivian Cate

Quinoa "Chicken" Stir Fry

Both Bob and Ryan enjoy cooking stir fry. No two preparations are alike! This recipe is one of Bob's earliest. Remember that quinoa is a great source of protein in addition to "chicken strips." When stir frying, start with firmer vegetables like onions, garlic, broccoli and carrots. Then add softer items like bell pepper and mushrooms.

Garlic oil (Trader Joe's)
1 medium to large onion, diced
1 bell pepper, diced
1 package shredded broccoli and carrots
2 stalks celery, chopped
Chopped greens (spinach, mustard greens, and/or kale)
8 ounces mushrooms
2 cloves garlic, minced
Trader Joe's "Chicken Strips"
1 cup quinoa

Mix 1 part quinoa to 2 ½ parts water and cook until thick. Set aside. Stir fry vegetables in oil until tender. Add "chicken" at the end and cook until warm. Melt butter substitute and sprinkle with lemon pepper OR season to taste with various herbs and spices (oregano, rosemary, thyme, sage, and basil) or Mrs. Dash original. Serve over quinoa.

Rock Island Jambalaya

Our sons Nick and Ryan were involved in Boy Scouts. Every other year, Troop 55 went to Rock Island for summer camp. This jambalaya was a

Vegan Cuisine

favorite meal. When we changed to a plant based diet, I adjusted all of our favorite recipes.

2 cups rice blend (or blend of white, brown, wild, and red rice)
2 8-ounce packages imitation chicken (chicken strips, seitan, or Boca nuggets)
1 package Tofurky Italian Sausage (4 links)
½ cup Earth Balance butter substitute
½ cup chopped parsley
1 package onion soup mix
1 package vegetable soup mix (or equivalent)
4 cups water
8 ounce can tomato sauce
1 bunch green onions, chopped
2 bay leaves
1 medium green pepper, chopped
1 Tablespoon thyme
1 teaspoon lemon pepper
¼ teaspoon cayenne pepper

For Scouts and those with the equipment, mix ingredients and cook in a Dutch oven with 8 hot coals underneath and 12 hot coals on top of the lid. Cook for about 1 ½ hours, stirring once after 45 minutes. Others may cook in a 350 degree oven for an hour until rice is cooked and jambalaya is thickened.

Sausage and Kraut

Mother learned very little of her father's Pennsylvania Dutch German dialect, but she did remember some great recipes from our ancestors. One was Sand Tarts (a flat sugar cookie containing nutmeg and cinnamon and topped with whipped egg white and a pecan). Another was Sausage and Kraut. When I discovered the sweet flavor of <u>Bavarian</u> sauerkraut blended with Tofurky <u>Italian</u> Sausage, this dish almost became a weekly request by my husband.

1/2 package (2 links) Tofurky Italian Sausage, sliced in 1/2 inch thick circles
1 15oz. can Bavarian sauerkraut (Kroger brand, but there are recipes online to make your own)
(optional) 1 Tbsp. Basil

Add ingredients together and simmer for 10-15 minutes. Serve with side of mashed red potatoes to which almond milk and Earth Balance butter have been added.

Sausage Patties

1 lb. Lightlife Gimme Lean sausage
¾ cup oatmeal (uncooked)
¾ cup pearl barley (cooked)
2 Tbsp. Bolner's Fiesta Brand Pan Sausage Seasoning (from Academy Sports)
¼ tsp. garlic powder

Mix all ingredients together and pat onto cutting board 1 ½ inch thick. Form into patties using a 2 inch biscuit cutter. Fry in lightly greased pan until brown on each side. Serve with **Bob's Biscuits** and jelly!

Stir Fry

Now that Bob seasons stir fry instead of steaks, we purchase large packages of stir fry mix from Costco. Our favorite contains baby corn, water chestnuts, huge mushrooms, uncut green beans. NOTE: if leftover salad starts to brown, add it to stir fry! For a burst of flavor, add the zest (grated skin) of a lemon or orange to soups and stir fries! Zest freezes well.

<u>Option #1: Basic Stir Fry</u>

2-3 cups mixed vegetables (onion, green pepper, mushrooms, coleslaw mix or shredded cabbage and carrots, kale and/or spinach, Bok Choy, squash)

(Optional) 1 can of beans and/or ¼ cup chopped almonds

Mrs. Dash Original, lemon pepper, or choice of seasonings (1-3 tsp. each)

Fry vegetables in small amount of oil or water until tender. Season to taste and add beans and/or almonds. Serve over rice or quinoa.

<u>Option #2: Oriental Stir Fry</u>

2 cups Basic Stir Fry
Chow Mein noodles
Soy Sauce (to taste)

Stir fry vegetables and serve over crunchy noodles. Season with soy sauce.

Vivian Cate

Option #3 Stir Fry Spaghetti

1 jar Spaghetti Sauce
2-4 cups left over Basic Stir Fry
(Optional) Additional garlic, oregano, basil to taste

Mix spaghetti sauce, stir fry, and seasonings. Warm and serve over cooked noodles

Stroganoff

Early in their marriage, my dad attended college to obtain his master's degree. They didn't have much money so they lived in a trailer park where Mother cleaned in exchange for rent and stretched their dollars by turning leftover roast into mouth-watering beef stroganoff. My version is healthier but still tasty!

4 oz. fresh mushrooms (diced) or 1 cup dried Shitake mushrooms
1 large onion (chopped)
1 pkg. seitan (cut into bite size pieces) or vegan "beef" substitute
½ c. Earth Balance butter substitute
3 Tbsp 100% whole wheat flour
¾ c. vanilla almond milk
Rice, quinoa, or noodles

Sautee onion in 1-2 Tbsps. safflower oil, add mushrooms and sauté, then add beef substitute and set aside. Melt butter and add flour. Slowly blend in milk. Stir until thickened and mix with vegetables. Serve over cooked rice, quinoa, or corn noodles.

Vegan Cuisine

Stuffed Green Peppers

1 ½ cups water
½ cup rice (red, wild, black blend)
5 large or 7 medium green peppers
12 oz. pkg. vegan ground crumbles
1 can diced tomatoes (or 4 large tomatoes, diced)
7 oz. pkg. Daiya grated vegan cheddar cheese
1 small onion, diced
6 oz. mushrooms, chopped
1 tsp lemon pepper
1 tsp. garlic powder
¼ tsp. red pepper
(Optional) 1 tsp. sage OR taco seasoning

Cook water and rice together until water is absorbed and rice is tender. Meanwhile, cut out tops from green peppers (set aside) and boil peppers in water for 4-5 minutes. Mix remaining ingredients together. Remove seed centers from green pepper tops and discard. Chop remaining green pepper from tops and add to other ingredients. Drain boiled peppers and place in deep casserole dish. Stuff each pepper to overflowing with mixture of ingredients. Bake in 350 degree oven for 25-30 minutes. This can be frozen.

Taco Cabbage and "Beef" Casserole

This has long been one of our favorite casseroles. I made a few changes to remove animal products and it tastes even better than before! Be encouraged to "veganize" your <u>own</u> family recipes!

Vivian Cate

1 ½ c. hash brown potatoes
½ c. shredded cheddar cheese substitute (we like Daiya)
¼ tsp. onion salt or garlic salt
¼ tsp. lemon pepper
1 lb. vegan "meat" crumbles
1 ½ c. shredded cabbage or coleslaw mix
¾ c. taco sauce
Onion salt and pepper
1 c. shredded cheddar cheese substitute (Daiya)
Taco sauce

Mix potatoes, ½ c. cheese substitute, onion/garlic salt, and pepper. Press into bottom and sides of a 1 quart baking dish. Bake at 350 degrees for 20 minutes. Meanwhile, stir fry cabbage over high heat 2 to 3 minutes. Add meat crumbles, ½ c. taco sauce, salt, and pepper and spoon onto partially baked potato crust. Bake 20 minutes. Top with remaining cheese and bake 2 to 3 more minutes until cheese melts. Top with vegan sour cream and taco sauce to serve. Makes 4 to 5 servings. Freezes well if you want to double the recipe.

Taco "Chicken" and Rice Casserole

1 large onion (chopped)
1 tablespoon Earth Balance butter substitute or olive oil
1 cup brown and/or wild rice
2 cups water
1 ½ cup salsa (medium or hot)
12 oz. package frozen corn
15 oz. can black beans
16 oz. seitan (cut into small cubes) or chicken substitute

8 oz. package Daiya Pepper Jack Cheese
(Optional) Taco chips
(Optional) Vegan sour cream
(Optional) Guacamole or sliced avocado

Sautee onion in oil or butter substitute. Cook rice in water until tender. Mix all ingredients except for chips, sour cream, and guacamole. Pour into one 13 X 9 baking dish (or two 8X8 dishes and freeze one dish). Cook at 350 degrees for 20 minutes. Serve over taco chips. Top with sour cream and a tablespoon of guacamole or sliced avocado.

Tasty Tortilla Stack

Our family loves anything with even a remotely Mexican flair! This is so popular that my original recipe is yellow from use!

¼ c safflower oil
8 large (8 inch) whole wheat tortillas
8oz. vegan sour cream (Tofutti)
1 cup medium salsa
8 oz. package vegan "chicken strips"
8 oz. package Daiya shredded cheddar cheese
4-5 minced green onions
2 tbsp. vegan butter (Earth Balance) melted
1 c. shredded lettuce
½ c. chopped tomato

Heat oil in 10 inch skillet. Fry each tortilla on medium high until crisp (about 10-15 seconds per side); drain on paper towels. Combine sour cream, salsa, cheese, onions, and "chicken." In a 13 X 9 inch lightly greased baking dish, start two stacks by placing two tortillas side by side. Spread each tortilla with mixture. Top with second tortillas and more sour cream mix. Add third tortillas to each stack and cover with remaining mixture. Cover with 4th tortillas and brush with melted butter. Warm in oven preheated at 350 degrees for 20 minutes. Top with lettuce and tomato.

Traditional Spaghetti

This is a vegan form of spaghetti. There are also a variety of packaged vegan meatballs that can be used in place of meat crumbles.

1 can spaghetti sauce (we prefer Heart Healthy Ragu)
1 package vegan meat crumbles (such as Boca)
8 ounces mushrooms, chopped
1 large onion, diced
(Optional) Additional garlic, oregano, basil to taste
Sam Mills 100% Corn Pasta OR spaghetti squash

Sautee onion and mushrooms. Blend with spaghetti sauce, meat crumbles, and seasonings until warm. Serve over noodles (cooked in water until softened) or spaghetti squash (cut in half, place on a cookie sheet with insides facing down, and bake at 350 degrees for 30-45 minutes. Use a fork to shred insides from cooked squash).

FRUIT SIDE DISHES

Cranberry Relish

OK I admit it … this is not totally vegan. It contains gelatin, which is an animal product. However, this recipe was given to me 40 years ago by a fellow nurse at Vanderbilt Hospital, and it soon became my "required" dish for Thanksgiving and Christmas meals at Cate gatherings! It also reminds me of the old meat grinder my mother attached to the counter when grinding up nuts, cranberries, and other fruit to make THE best cranberry relish in town (and hers did <u>not</u> have gelatin!)

2 cups sugar
1 lb. package cranberries (halved or sliced in salad shooter)
1 cup crushed nuts (pecans or walnuts)
1 large can crushed pineapple (drained but save juice)
Zest of 1 orange (grated peel)
1 large or 2 small packages raspberry gelatin
(Optional) 1-2 grated apples

Pour raspberry gelatin into ONE cup boiling water, add ONE cup cold liquid which consists of pineapple juice and water (package calls for two of each). Add all other ingredients and blend together. Refrigerate eight (8) hours or overnight to set.

Fruit Salad

What's in your pantry? What's in the produce drawer of your frig? Throw together whatever fruit you have on hand, toss in some nuts, and blend with this quick and easy sauce for a dish that begs for second helpings!

2 fresh bananas
1 can peaches (and/or pears)

1 can mandarin oranges
2 apples
Handful of grapes
1 container coconut, almond, or soy yogurt (any flavor)
2 tablespoons wildflower honey or maple syrup
1-2 teaspoons cinnamon (nutmeg also adds great flavor)
2 teaspoons almond or vanilla extract
Toasted almonds, walnuts, or pecans

Slice bananas, drain and cut fruit into bite size pieces, and mix together in large bowl. Blend yogurt, honey or maple syrup, cinnamon, and extract together and fold into fruit. Add seeds or nuts as desired.

Granny's Favorite Ambrosia

I was blessed to have a wonderful mother-in-law! Granny was a fabulous artist who never sold her work but shared among her family. When I first met her, I called her "Mom" as if my spirit knew she would become my "other mother." Later, because she was so short, I called her my "half pint Momma!" A friend who was fairly well endowed once commented, "Well, then, I guess that makes me your full quart Momma!"

Granny was especially important to me because my own mother died when I was 29 years old, five years before I met and married Bob. When the kids came along, said their first words, sprouted a tooth, started to walk or any one of their other antics, Granny was the one I called. She always had a word of joyful praise and encouragement. Even when she no longer recognized us, Granny would express her deep thanks for every little thing I did for her. One of the foods for which Granny was especially thankful was Pappy's Ambrosia!

15 ounce can mandarin oranges (well drained)
6 ounce jar maraschino cherries (well drained)
29 ounce can fruit cocktail, pears, or peaches (well drained)
1 banana (sliced)
½ cup coconut
(Optional) ½ cup small marshmallows
(Optional) ½ cup pineapple
(Optional) walnuts or pecans
¼ cup Vegenaise

Mix all ingredients together and serve. Instead of fruit cocktail, use pears, peaches, grapes, apples, and other fresh fruit.

Pappy's Pear and Peanut Butter Side Dish

When we married, I quit nursing to work with Bob in his landscape business, Nature's Place, Inc. Many of our customers lived within a few miles of his parents' home, so once a week we'd stop by. Regardless of the time of day, Pappy's first words were normally, "Let me get you something to eat!" Pappy often served Ambrosia, but this was his backup!

2-3 pear halves
1-2 Tbsp. peanut butter (smooth or crunchy)
Lettuce
1 tsp. Vegenaise

Place pears in refrigerator to cool. Lay 2-3 pear halves on a bed of lettuce. Scoop a heaping tablespoon of peanut butter onto pears, and top with a teaspoon of Vegenaise.

Vivian Cate

Peach Chutney

*Remember the 55-60 gallons of dried peaches that I bought (see **Almond Peach Pie**)? Here's another delicious recipe that came from that purchase!*

¾ cup cranberry juice
1 cup sugar
1 tsp. each of ground cinnamon and nutmeg
¼ tsp. each ground cloves and ginger
½ c. dried cranberries (or mixture of cranberries and raisins)
8 oz. bag cranberries
1 c. dried peaches (diced)
½ c. toasted pecans (chopped)
Zest (grated peel) of 1 orange

Boil juice, spices, and peaches. Add sugar and cranberries. Boil 3-5 minutes, add pecans and zest. Chill (lasts a week in refrigerator). Use as side dish or serve with vegan cream cheese and crackers.

SALADS & DRESSINGS

Chef Salads

Chef Salads were a quick and easy meal for days when I'd worked 12 hours seeing patients, doing paperwork, and making work-related phone calls (you have those days, too, don't you!) Add seasonal vegetables such as broccoli, squash, zucchini, or cauliflower. Try new vegetables like jicama (kind of like water chestnut with mild apple flavor) or one of the cabbages.

Option #1:

Mixed greens
1 bag coleslaw mix
1 green pepper, chopped
1/3 jicama, cut into bite-size pieces
1 large or 2 medium tomatoes, diced
1 can black beans, drained
1 can mandarin oranges, drained
Warm black beans. Mix with salad and serve with dressing.

Option #2:

Mixed greens
1 bag coleslaw mix
1 Cucumber, diced
1 package vegan deli ham (sandwich slices) or vegan chicken, chopped
½ cup walnuts or pecans, chopped
½ cup fresh strawberries, sliced

Toss ingredients together in large bowl. Serve with salad dressing.

Vivian Cate

Chinese Coleslaw

I not only like to cook, but I like to do it quickly! Why grate up a bunch of carrots and cabbage when you can buy the mix inexpensively! We use it in tossed salads, stir fries, and various types of coleslaws like this one!

1 pound coleslaw mix
¼ cup each of almonds and sunflower seeds
1 package Raman noodles (uncooked and without flavor package)
4 green onions (with green stems)
½ cup Vegenaise
¼ cup red wine vinegar
½ cup sugar (may use stevia)

Toast almonds, seeds, and noodles for 5 minutes in preheated oven at 350 degrees. Mix together all ingredients and enjoy!

Four Bean Salad

Mother used to make the best Four Bean Salad in the world. The key was her dressing. Surprisingly, her salad is just as good without the oil found in the original recipe.

1 can Green Beans, drained
1 can Wax Beans, drained
1 can Kidney Beans, drained
1 can Lima Beans, drained
1 onion, chopped
1-2 stalks celery, chopped

(optional) Green Pepper, chopped
2/3 cup Red Wine Vinegar
2/3 cup sugar (may need more if using stevia)

Heat vinegar and sugar until sugar is dissolved. Toss all ingredients together. Store in a covered dish for several hours or overnight (the longer it sets, the more the beans soak up the sweet and sour flavor of the dressing). If I do not have them in the hydrator, I omit celery and/or green peppers.

Garbanzo Bean Salad

Make your own version of potato salad but switch the potatoes for garbanzo beans. If you prefer a more tart flavor, use dill pickles instead of bread and butter pickles.

1 can garbanzo beans (or chick peas), drained
2 stalks chopped celery
1/2 onion, diced
2 Tbsp. Dijon mustard
½ cup bread and butter pickles (drained and diced)
½ cup Vegenaise
Season with Mrs. Dash original and Lemon Pepper

Mix all ingredients and refrigerate several hours or overnight so that beans can absorb the flavors. May be served as a main dish!

Vivian Cate

Mandarin Quinoa Salad

Sometimes I create a new recipe from several others. Such was the case with this salad. One recipe had an especially good dressing using honey and ginger. Another recipe called for mangos which I replaced with mandarin oranges. I prefer cherry tomatoes to sliced tomatoes and the nutty texture of frozen corn in this particular salad. Be adventurous! Adjust recipes to your tastes!

1 cup quinoa
2 cups water
¾ cup cherry tomatoes, sliced in half
6 oz. frozen corn
1 cucumber, peeled and diced
15 oz. can mandarin oranges, drained
Chives (chopped greens) of 4 green onions
Zest (grated rind) and juice of 1 lemon
2 tsp. lemon pepper
½ - ¾ cup honey (to taste)
½ cup cashews
Spinach or Romaine lettuce

Bring quinoa and water to boil. Cover and reduce heat and simmer 10 to 15 minutes until quinoa is fluffy when turned with a fork. Add remaining ingredients and toss. Serve on bed on spinach or lettuce.

Noodled Garden Salad

I love having company for a meal, but, with our hectic schedule and lifestyle, it takes advanced planning. This can be made a day or two ahead of time …. the longer, the better! To turn this into a main dish, simply add one can of black beans and serve with muffins and a fruit salad. Note: these noodles may contain egg. You can substitute with Sam Mills corn noodles, quinoa pasta, or rice noodles.

1 package noodles with tomato, basil, and spinach flavors (cooked)
1 head chopped broccoli, cut into bite-size pieces
1 ½ cups baby carrots, diced
(Optional) Radishes, sliced
1 medium Vidalia onion, chopped
2/3 cup red wine vinegar
2/3 cup sugar (we use stevia)
6 ounces vegan Mozzarella (or 2-3 Tbsp. vegan Parmesan cheese)

Mix all ingredients together and refrigerate for several hours or overnight.

Orzo Salad

When my husband introduced me to the Olive Oil Store in Nashville, I balked at the enormous selection! Then the manager introduced me to their sample kit of three Balsamic vinegars with three flavored olive oils. I soon came up with some delicious and healthy recipes that can be stored for several days in the refrigerator.

8 oz. orzo, cooked
1 can black olives, cut in quarters
¾ cup carrots, diced
1 cucumber, chopped

¾ to 1 cup baby tomatoes, cut in half
1 sweet onion, chopped
½ cup pecans, chopped
(Optional) Green peppers, diced
3 Tbsp. Lemon fused olive oil (from Olive Oil Store)
3 Tbsp. Honey Ginger White Balsamic Vinegar (from Olive Oil Store)
2-3 tsp. Mrs. Dash Lemon Pepper

Blend ingredients together and store in refrigerator. Flavor improves by the hour!

Pasta Vegetable Salad

The great thing about pasta salads is that they can be made ahead for a luncheon, served as a side at dinner, or blended with a can of beans to stand on its own as a meal.

8oz. tomato spinach fusilli (or other pasta)
1 yellow squash, diced
1 zucchini, diced
1 small onion, diced
1 cup grape tomatoes, cut in halves
8 baby carrots, chopped
1 Tbsp. basil
¾ cup red wine vinegar
¾ cup sugar (or stevia)
(Optional) Vegan Parmesan cheese

Precook pasta until tender and drain thoroughly. Add remaining vegetables and basil. Over medium heat, dissolve sugar in vinegar. Then pour over pasta/vegetable mixture. Stir salad and store in refrigerator overnight. May sprinkle vegan Parmesan cheese over top before serving.

Pineapple Coleslaw

Bob and I discovered the Wild Cow, a vegetarian restaurant in East Nashville. One of their side dishes was pineapple coleslaw. This is our version of that dish to which we add raisins and cranberries for extra flavor!

1 bag of coleslaw mix (or make your own)
1 can crushed pineapple (thoroughly drained)
½ cup raisins and/or dried cranberries
4 Tbsp. Vegenaise
(Optional) ¼ cup sunflower seeds

Mix ingredients together and store in refrigerator until ready to serve.

Pomegranate Bean Salad

When my husband learned that the Olive Oil Store has a Pomegranate Balsamic Vinegar, he purchased a 12 ounce bottle!

1 can garbanzo beans
1 can black beans
12 ounce package frozen corn
12 ounce package frozen edamame beans
¼ cup Roasted Japanese Almond Oil (from Olive Oil Store)

¼ cup sugar or stevia
¼ cup Pomegranate Balsamic Vinegar (from Olive Oil Store)

Mix ingredients together and store in refrigerator 8 hours or overnight. Flavor improves with time. Serve cold as a side dish salad, heat and serve as an entrée over rice, or pour over mixed greens and vegetables for a chef salad.

Seitan Salad Stuffed Tomatoes

1 pkg seitan (wheat product) OR vegan "chicken"
½ cup chopped bread and butter pickles
2 stalks celery (diced)
2-3 tbsp. Vegenaise
2-3 tsp. curry
(Optional) Grapes and pecans
3-4 tomatoes

Cut seitan or "chicken" into bite size pieces or pulse briefly in food processor. Add remaining ingredients and chill for 30 minutes or more. Divide each tomato into four quarters and scoop a large spoonful of "chicken" salad into each center.

Taco Salad

Martha is "family", plain and simple! Since her husband Blake's death, she has blessed our home on Wednesday evenings. Normally I prepare the main meal and Martha brings a large salad. She generously leaves leftovers which Bob and I turn into **Taco Salad** *on Fridays! (There* *are no vegetable measurements in this salad! Just use what is in your refrigerator ... a handful of greens, a couple of carrots, a few slices of each pepper, a leftover piece of squash!)*

Mixed greens
Carrots, grated
Grape tomatoes, halved
Cucumber, diced
Green, yellow, and/or red pepper, chopped
Radishes
Avocado, mashed or chopped
1 can black beans, drained
½ cup vegan sour cream
½ cup salsa
Taco chips

Warm beans for 1 minute in microwave. Mix salad ingredients and serve on bed of mildly crushed Taco chips. Mix sour cream and salsa together and pour over salad.

Vegetable Couscous Salad

2/3 cup couscous
1 ¼ cup water
4 Tbsp. red wine vinegar
½ cup stevia
2 Tbsp. soy sauce (we use Bragg's)
Zest and juice of 1 lemon
1 medium zucchini (with skin, cut in half and thinly slice)
1 small to medium yellow squash (with skin, cut in half and thinly slice)

1 medium to large cucumber (remove skin, cut in quarters and slice)
2 green onions (dice onion and greens)
1/3 jicama or 1 can water chestnuts (diced)
1 cup grape tomatoes (halved)
2 tsp. lemon pepper
(Optional) 1 can black beans or garbanzo/chickpea beans (drained)

Stir couscous into boiling water, cover and set aside for 3-4 minutes. Blend vinegar, stevia, soy sauce, and lemon. Mix vegetables together and add couscous. Fold in vinegar sauce and refrigerate for one to two hours (the longer it sets, the more the vegetables absorb the flavor!) To add protein and make this a meal in itself, add one can of beans.

Barbeque French Dressing

Sometimes recipes develop just because we have a "hankering" for something different! Bob is always saying, "all this needs is a little barbeque sauce!" We enjoy this spicy dressing on tossed salads or as a dip for Sausage Wraps.

1 cup sugar (or stevia)
1/3 c barbeque sauce
1/3 c. catsup
1/2 c. rice, balsamic, or white vinegar

Mix all ingredients and heat until sugar is dissolved (if using stevia, it does not need to be heated). If dressing seems too thick, add a small amount of water. Cool and store in refrigerator.

Cucumber Dressing

Some families like a variety of salad dressings. We have different colored tops for each salad dressing!

2 medium to large cucumbers (peeled and seeds removed)
8 oz. Tofutti cream cheese
2 Tsp. Vegenaise
2 cloves fresh garlic, minced
4 Tbsp. fresh chopped chives (the stems of green onions)
3 Tbsp. dill, chopped
2 tsp. black pepper
2/3 cup almond milk

Place cucumbers in food processor and pulse. Add remaining ingredients and refrigerate overnight so flavors are more enhanced. Store in sealed container.

French Dressing

While oil adds a smoothness to salad dressings, it is not necessary to add more oil than is already in the ingredients. Instead, add natural oils from avocados and nuts to salads. I saw a French dressing recipe that called for one cup of oil and only 2 Tablespoons catsup! Immediately I threw together the following.

1 ½ cup Vegenaise
1 cup catsup
1/3 cup red wine vinegar
2 Tablespoon stevia (or sugar)
1 Tablespoon Mrs. Dash Lemon Pepper

Mix together or use shaker made for salad dressings. If dressing seems too thick, add a small amount of vanilla almond milk. Store in refrigerator.

Red Wine Vinegar Dressing

Many years ago I found a recipe for salad. It included lettuce, mandarin oranges, and toasted almonds with an oil, vinegar, and sugar dressing. I eventually modified the dressing to eliminate oil. This keeps for weeks in the refrigerator and can be used on any kind of salad.

1 cup red wine vinegar
1 cup sugar (or stevia)

Stir over heat until sugar is melted. Cool, pour into a glass jar with a lid, and store in the refrigerator.

Vivian's Ranch Dressing

I love Ranch Dressing! This dressing is easy to make and every bit as good as what you buy in the store. Note that Mrs. Dash is not only salt-free, but it also contains less pepper than some brands.

1 ½ cup Vegenaise
2 Tbsp. Mrs. Dash Original seasoning
1 Tbsp. Mrs. Dash Lemon Pepper (other brands have salt)

½ c. vanilla almond milk
(Optional) ¼ cup Tofutti sour cream

Shake and store in refrigerator for up to two weeks. Adjust the amount of milk to fit your desired thickness.

SANDWICHES

American Grilled Burgers

Our favorites burgers are Boca's American Grilled Burger and the Chipotle Black Bean Burger by Morningstar (which is vegetarian because it contains egg and milk). Load each burger bun like you would a traditional burger (Vegenaise, mustard, tomato, lettuce, onion, pickle) OR try the following!

1 green pepper
1 onion
1 Tbsp. oil (or ¼ cup water)
Burgers
(Optional) Sliced tomatoes
(Optional) Leaf of lettuce
Whole wheat burger buns

Sautee diced green pepper and onion in oil or water until soft. Grill burgers and warm buns. Serve sautéed vegetables on burgers in buns. Add condiments as desired.

BLT Sandwich

Some things never change ... like our love for bacon, lettuce, and tomato sandwiches! Bob and I both grew up on these.

2 slices Texas toast
1-2 Tbsp. Vegenaise
1-2 tsp. mustard
2 strips vegan bacon
Garlic powder
1-2 slices fresh tomato

(Optional) 1 slice vegan cheddar or jalapeno cheese
1 large leaf of crisp lettuce
Earth Balance butter substitute

Fry bacon in small amount of oil. Sprinkle with garlic powder. Spread Vegenaise and mustard on 2 slices of Texas toast. Layer bacon, tomato, cheese, and lettuce on one slice of bread and cover with second slice. Serve as is or spread outer bread with butter substitute and grill both sides until lightly browned.

Bumble Bean Burritos

My motto is "waste not, want not." Think about it! The more you save, the more you have to give! Instead of throwing away food, freeze and reuse in a different way ... like these burritos!

Leftover **Bumble Bean Stew** (see recipe)
1 package large wheat tortillas
Daiya cheese (crumbled cheddar or melted Jalapeno)
Avocado, sliced
Tofutti Sour Cream

Place 3-4 Tablespoons of Bumble Bean Stew down center of each tortilla and top with cheese. Turn bottom of tortilla up over beginning strip of beans. Roll sides over strip of beans and each other. Place side-by-side in 9X13 dish and place in oven set at 350 degrees for 30 minutes. Top each burrito with a "dollup" of sour cream and slices of avocado! Serve with side dishes of rice and fruit.

Chik-N-Salad Sandwich

Turn leftovers into delicious lunches! Add a side of sweet potato tots or fries and top off the meal with fresh fruit!

2 slices whole wheat bread
3-4 tablespoons **Chik-N-Salad** (see recipe)
1 slice tomato
1 leaf Romaine lettuce

Toast two slices of bread. Spread one slice with **Chik-N-Salad**. Layer with tomato and lettuce and cover with second slice of bread.

Cucumber Spread Sandwich

A popular "open house" delicacy is cucumber sandwiches. This recipe contains the same food items but in a way that is tasty, attractive, and easier to eat. Once sandwiches are placed on a platter, sparsely toss parsley flakes across the top!

1 large cucumber (best if peeled and seeds removed)
8 oz. Tofutti cream cheese
2 Tsp. Vegenaise
2 cloves fresh garlic, minced
4 Tbsp. fresh chopped chives (the stems of green onions)
3 Tbsp. dill, chopped
2 tsp. black pepper

Place cucumbers in food processor and pulse. Add remaining ingredients and refrigerate overnight so flavors are more enhanced. Cover slice of whole wheat bread with healthy amount of spread. Top with second slice of bread.

Eggless Salad Sandwich

1 tub extra firm tofu
1 tsp. soy sauce
2 stalks celery, chopped
2 tsp. lemon juice
1 tsp. lemon pepper
1/3 cup sweet pickle relish
¼ onion, diced
1 tbsp. Dijon mustard
(Optional) Italian herbs to taste

Crumble tofu and add remaining ingredients. Mustard gives flavor as well as color, but a little turmeric can also be added for color. This sandwich is especially good with slices of avocado on each slice of bread before loading with Eggless Salad.

Lemon Cumato Sandwich

I grew up eating cucumber sandwiches! The lemon juice and lemon pepper enhance the flavors while tomatoes give a meatier texture!

Cucumber (washed & with peel left on)
Tomato slices
Vegenaise (to taste)

2-3 tsp. lemon juice
Lemon Pepper (no salt variety)

Wash cucumbers. Leave peel on and slice into ¼ to ½ inch circles. Spread 2 slices whole wheat bread with Vegenaise. Cover one slice of bread with four cucumber circles. Pour lemon juice over cucumbers and sprinkle with Mrs. Dash Lemon Pepper. Cover with second slice of bread and cut into squares.

Meatless Loaf Sandwich

Option #1:

2 slices whole wheat bread, toasted
Vegenaise
Slice of tomato
Leave of lettuce
Leftover **Meatless Loaf** (optional)
Lemon pepper

Spread Vegenaise on both inner slices of toasted whole wheat bread. Layer tomato and ¼ inch layer meatloaf on first slice. Cover with second slice of toast!

Option #2:

2 slices whole wheat bread, toasted
Barbeque sauce
Vidalia onion, thinly sliced
Leftover **Meatless Loaf**

Spread barbeque sauce on both inner slices of toasted whole wheat bread. Layer onion and ¼ inch layer meatloaf on first slice. Cover with second slice of toast and enjoy!

OLT Sandwich

People often ask how we can "eat out" if we are vegans. Creatively, that's how! Bob stopped at a local establishment one day and wanted a BLT (bacon, lettuce, and tomato) sandwich. Obviously he did not want the bacon so he asked if it could be traded for crispy onion rings. That's when the OLT (onion, lettuce and tomato) sandwich was birthed!

2 slices Texas toast (or whole wheat bun)
1-2 Tbsp. Vegenaise
1-2 tsp. mustard
Sliced bread and butter pickles
3 fried onion rings (frozen breaded onion rings)
1-2 slices fresh tomato
1 large leaf of crisp lettuce
Earth Balance butter substitute

Bake onion rings in oven according to package instructions. Spread Vegenaise and mustard on 2 slices Texas toast. Layer onion rings, lettuce, pickles, and tomato on one slice of bread and cover with second slice. Serve as is or grill both sides until lightly browned. Serve with Sweet Potato Crinkles or Fries (prepared according to package directions).

Pig in a Blanket with Mustard Sauce

4 vegan hot dogs
1 tube (8) jumbo biscuits (or dough for 8 homemade biscuits)
2/3 cup Vegenaise
1/3 cup mustard

Cut hotdogs in half. Wrap each half in a biscuit, sealing the edges together. Bake for 10 to 12 minutes at 350 degrees. Serve with mixture of Vegenaise and mustard. We keep hot dogs in the freezer and biscuits in the refrigerator for this quick and easy lunch or dinner. They also taste good cold for breakfast!

Pimento Cheese Sandwich

8 oz. package Daiya cheese
½ to 3/4 cup bread & butter pickles, diced
2 stalks celery, chopped
4 oz. jar pimento
1/3 cup Vegenaise
Lemon pepper

Blend ingredients. Melt for 1 minute on high in microwave and stir. Serve in sandwiches, with crackers, or with raw vegetables.

Sausage Wraps

1 box Boca sausage links (10 per pack)
1 tube jumbo biscuits (8 to container) or homemade biscuit dough
(Optional) Barbecue sauce or honey

Divide each biscuit in half, flatten, and wrap one sausage link in each biscuit half. Place on cookie sheet and bake at 350 degrees until biscuits turn medium brown (about 10 to 12 minutes). These are delicious as is but can also be dipped in barbecue sauce, honey, or butter substitute.

Sloppy Joes

1 package meat crumbles
1 onion, diced
1 clove garlic, minced
1 Tbsp. oil
4 ounces mushrooms
½ cup Hickory flavored barbecue sauce
Whole Wheat hamburger buns or Deli buns
Butter substitute
Garlic powder

Sautee onion, garlic, and mushrooms in oil. Add meat crumbles and barbecue sauce to moisten. Cook on medium heat for 5 minutes. Butter the buns, sprinkle with garlic powder, and broil for 3 to 4 minutes. Spoon desired amount of Sloppy Joe mix onto toasted buns and serve with **Pineapple Coleslaw** and sweet potato fries or puffs.

Vegan Cuisine

Spinach Burgers

On a rare occasion, Bob and I will "stray" a little from our vegan diet. This is one of our exceptions due to the fact that you cannot beat the flavor of feta cheese in these burgers!

1 cup herb flavored dried stuffing
½ cup feta cheese crumbles (dairy product)
1 teaspoon lemon pepper
1 teaspoon oregano
1 to 2 cloves minced garlic (to taste)
3 tablespoons Ener-G Egg Replacer
¼ cup water
1 package (10 ounces) frozen chopped spinach
4 deli buns or whole wheat burger buns

Thaw and drain spinach. Mix all ingredients together and form into patties. Heat oil in pan and add patties. Cook until brown (about 3 to 4 minutes per side). Spread Vegenaise on warmed buns, and add patties, lettuce, tomato slices, and even a slice of Vidalia onion.

Stir Fry Burgers

Bob and I could eat these every day! They are D-LICIOUS and practically melt in your mouth!

Leftover stir fry
1 Deli bun (which may have egg) or whole wheat burger bun
1 slice vegan pepper jack cheese
Garlic and lemon pepper

Open and butter deli burger buns and generously sprinkle with garlic and lemon pepper. Toast in oven. Place slice of vegan pepper jack cheese on each bun, and fill with left over warmed stir fry. Serve with sweet potato fries.

Stir Fry Burritos

1 large whole wheat tortilla
Leftover stir fry
Vegan sour cream
Salsa

Warm tortillas to make them more moldable. Heat left over stir fry and spoon portions down center of each tortilla. Fold one end up 1 ½ to 2 inches to form the bottom of the burrito. Fold right third of tortilla towards center to cover strip of stir fry and then left third of tortilla in to cover right flap. Burritos may be warmed in oven or microwave if necessary. Serve with salsa and a spoonful of vegan sour cream!

SOUPS

Amanda's Taco Soup

Not long after Bob and I changed to a plant based diet, we learned that our daughter Amanda had also begun making the change. We have had fun over the years, sharing recipes with each other! This is Amanda's, and she even taught me how to make tortilla strips to go on top!

2 cans tomatoes with Jalapeno peppers
4 cans beans (such as black, pinto, garbanzo, kidney)
1 package low salt taco seasoning
1 package dry ranch dressing (or ½ cup **Vivian's Ranch Dressing**)
2 cans vegetable stock (or equivalent)
1 cup frozen corn (or use whole package)
1 cup onion, diced
1 Tbsp. garlic powder
(Optional) 16 ounces fresh mushrooms

Mix in crockpot and cook for 4 hours on low. Top with tortilla strips.

Tortilla Strips

Slice tortillas into strips with pizza cutter. Lightly oil and bake at 350 degrees until crunchy.

Broccoli Soup

We do not care for watery soups. This method of thickening is quick and easy.

1 tablespoons oil
3-4 stalks diced celery
1 cup diced carrots
1 diced onion
4-6 oz. mushrooms, diced
1 large head of broccoli (or 1 package broccoli florets), diced
1 package vegetable broth mix (or 1 can vegetable broth)
1 ½ quarts water (minus 1 cup if using canned broth)
1 cup almond milk (may use coconut or soy milk creamer)
(Optional) 1 cup Daiya Jalapeno cheese

Sautee celery, carrots, and onion in oil until onion becomes translucent. Add mushrooms and sauté until tender. Stir in broccoli and cook 5 minutes longer. Pour in water and simmer over medium heat for 15-30 minutes. Puree half of the soup in blender or food processor. Return to chunky vegetables and add milk. If extra seasoning needed, add lemon pepper to taste.

Butternut Squash Soup

Butternut squash is delicious in succotash (see recipe), can be cooked and eaten as is with a little butter and pepper, or used to thicken soups (cook and mash, then add to any recipe of soup). Butternut squash also makes a tasty soup on its own.

1 large butternut squash
¼ cup vegan butter substitute
Pepper or lemon pepper
Vanilla almond milk

Cut squash in half and bake at 400 degrees for about 45 minutes (until tender). Remove skin and mash or process in blender, adding milk, butter, and pepper until desired consistency obtained.

Cashew Cream

½ cup cashews soaked in 2 tbsp. water
Vanilla almond milk
(Optional) Pureed date paste, lemon juice and vanilla extract OR orange juice OR herbs and spices for additional flavor.

Soak cashews in water for at least 30 minutes or overnight. Puree cashews, adding milk as needed. **Cashew Cream** can be prepared in larger quantities, molded into ½ cup servings, and frozen in a Ziploc bag for later soups, casseroles, desserts, fruit salads, or sandwich spreads.

"Chicken" Vegetable Soup

*Add **Cashew Cream** to thicken this soup and give it extra protein.*

1 onion
8 ounces mushrooms

1 to 1 ½ cups kidney beans
1 cup carrots
1 cup Corn
1 cup green beans
1 cup edamame
1 package seitan chunks
Mrs. Dash original blend (to taste)
Lemon pepper (to taste)
4 ounces Cashew Cream

In a small amount of oil, sauté chopped onion. When translucent, add chopped mushrooms. Cook fresh or frozen vegetables in water. Add Cashew Cream, onions, mushrooms, and seasoning.

Creamy Curried Potato Soup

1 onion, chopped
1 large carrot, grated
3 cloves garlic, minced
15 ounce can diced tomatoes (with liquid)
1 zucchini, sliced
5 large red or golden potatoes, cut into chunks
1 ½ cup vegetable broth
2 tsp. cinnamon
1 ½ tsp. cumin
1 tsp. turmeric
2 tsp. curry
1 cup almond milk
1 tsp. lemon pepper

Place all ingredients in large lidded pot and simmer until fork goes through vegetables (about 30 minutes). Place ½ of soup in blender or food processor and pulse to puree. Return to pot with chunky vegetables. Serve with crispy thin wheat crackers.

Hearty Soup

Sometimes simple is better. Don't underestimate the power of Ro-Tel Mexican Lime and Cilantro tomatoes plus Mrs. Dash seasoning in this soup!

1 can northern beans with juice
1 can black beans with juice
1 can or small pkg. frozen corn
Other assorted vegetables such as okra, diced carrots, green beans, onions
2 cans Ro-Tel Mexican Lime and Cilantro tomatoes
3 Tbsp. Mrs. Dash seasoning or spices to taste

Mix ingredients together, add water if needed, warm, and serve with crackers or homemade bread. Freeze half of this recipe for another meal.

Mushroom Soup

A number of our recipes call for mushroom soup. I also use this in the popular green bean casserole with mushroom soup and dried onion rings.

½ cup Earth Balance butter substitute
2 Tablespoons whole wheat flour
1 cup almond milk
4 ounces fresh mushrooms
Mrs. Dash original and/or Mrs. Dash lemon pepper to taste

Slice mushrooms and sauté in small amount of oil. Melt butter and blend in flour. Slowly add milk while stirring. Add mushrooms and cook until thickened. This can be used in green bean casserole, broccoli casserole, cream soups, and other recipes calling for mushroom soup.

Split Pea Soup

1 package dried split peas
½ to 1 cup almond milk
1 tsp. garlic powder
1 tbsp. soy sauce
1 tsp. curry
1 cup cooked rice, quinoa, or pearl barley

Boil package of split peas in water according to package directions. When tender, process in blender, adding almond milk to desired consistency. Season with garlic, soy sauce, and curry (add more if desired). Serve with pretzels OR add a cup of cooked rice, quinoa, or pearl barley. Freeze leftovers.

Tortilla Soup

1 large or 2 small zucchini
1 large can crushed tomatoes
6 cups vegetable broth
1 15oz. can hominy, garbanzo beans, black beans, corn, chick peas, or mixture
1 ½ tsp. cumin (or more)
½ tsp. cayenne pepper (or red pepper)
Cilantro to taste
(optional) seitan, cubed (in lieu of chicken)

Sautee zucchini for about 2 minutes, add other ingredients and boil. Then simmer 15 to 20 minutes. This soup has enough protein that it can be served without seitan (especially for those with gluten intolerance). Top with Tofutti sour cream, sliced avocados, Daiya cheese alternative. Serve over tortilla chips.

VEGETABLE SIDE DISHES

Asparagus Risotto

1 lb. asparagus
2 pkg. Knoll's vegetable mix
6 cups water
2 Tbsp. coconut oil (or olive oil)
2 medium onions, chopped
8 oz. fresh mushrooms, sliced
1 ½ cup blended rice (wild, red, white, brown)
¼ cup A-1 Sauce
Black pepper to taste
6 oz. frozen corn
6 oz. frozen spinach
¼ to ½ cup grated Parmesan cheese (we use a vegetarian parmesan)

Boil vegetable mix in 6 cups water. Remove woody ends from asparagus and place remaining vegetables in dish with lid. Microwave 1 ½ minutes; then set aside. Sautee onions. Stir in mushrooms and cook until tender. Add uncooked rice, steak sauce, and 1 cup of vegetable broth. Cook until most of liquid has been absorbed and add another cup of broth. Continue this pattern of cooking and adding broth until all broth has been used. Blend in corn and spinach and cook 2 minutes before adding asparagus. When most of liquid is absorbed, stir in Parmesan cheese and simmer 1 to 2 more minutes. This process takes about 30 minutes and rice will be a tad "nutty" in texture. Asparagus also adds a "nutty" texture to this dish!

Vivian Cate

Baked Summer Squash

We rarely add salt to foods. There is natural salt in many foods plus we prefer lemon pepper. Surprisingly, the lemon gives food a salty taste!

3 lb. yellow summer squash
2 onions
½ cup butter substitute
1 tsp. horseradish
1 Tbsp. Worcestershire sauce
½ tsp. garlic
¾ tsp. lemon pepper
¾ cup almond milk
1 cup mushroom soup (see recipe in this book)
4 Tbsp. Ener-G Egg Replacer
1 cup Herbal stuffing mix or crushed Ritz crackers
1 cup Daiya cheddar cheese (block)

Cook squash and onions in small amount of water. Drain and add remaining ingredients except for cheese stuffing mix/crackers. Alternate squash mix with stuffing mix, crackers. Bake at 400 degrees for 30 minutes.

Basil Zucchini

1 large zucchini
4 large tomatoes (or a 28 ounce can tomatoes)
1 Tablespoon basil
¼ cup sugar or ½ cup stevia

Peel and slice zucchini. Cook on stove in small amount of water. Add tomatoes and continue to cook until vegetables are soft. Blend in basil and sweetener. This is delicious hot or cold!

Beverly's Cinnamon Sweet Potatoes

I was never fond of sweet potatoes ... until my South Carolina friend Beverly (who is an awesome professional ventriloquist) introduced me to this delicious recipe! Pecans can be added for texture and extra flavor.

2 medium sweet potatoes (try purple Japanese variety for even more nutrients)
½ cup brown sugar
½ cup Earth Balance butter substitute
2-4 tsp. cinnamon

Cook sweet potatoes in the oven or microwave. Remove peel and mash with brown sugar, butter, and cinnamon.

Broccoli Casserole

2 cups rice blend
1 can drained chopped water chestnuts or bite size slices of jicama
2 cups **Mushroom Soup** (see recipe)
1 24-32 ounce package broccoli, cooked and drained
1 8-ounce package Daiya cheddar cheese (block)
2 tsp. lemon pepper

Cook rice as directed on package. Melt Daiya cheese for 1 minute in microwave. Blend all ingredients together, pour into casserole dish, and cook at 350 degrees for 30 minutes or until warm throughout.

Butternut Succotash

Mother cooked for large political campaigns as well as smaller dinner parties in her home. I loved her succotash, made with creamed corn, lima beans, and butter. One day, I found a new type of succotash. To my surprise, butternut squash adds sweetness to recipes!

1 butternut squash
1 pkg. frozen corn
1 pkg. frozen baby lima beans
Earth Balance to taste
Pepper

Slice squash in half and cook in oven at 400 degrees for 45 minutes or microwave until medium tenderness. Scoop out squash into bite-size chunks. Add corn, lima beans, Earth Balance, and pepper. Simmer until warm.

Can't Believe It's Turnips

When Bob and I married, we rented a hundred acre farm complete with neighbor's cows! One day this city girl came home to find Aida in the front yard. "BOB!" I said over the phone. "There's a cow in the yard!" He told me to shew her back into the fenced area! "But it's BIG!" Bob came home!

Later, while mowing the front field, my stomach became queasy. "BOB! It's like someone's cooking turnips." (I have never been able to eat, smell, or even be around the cooking of turnips). Bob laughed as he pointed to the field of yellow flowers. "Aren't they beautiful!" I exclaimed. Still chuckling, Bob stated, "Those, my dear, are turnips!"

I never mastered shewing cows back into the fenced area, but I did learn to eat the milder turnips used in this recipe!

3 purple top turnips
1 can chick peas/garbanzo beans
¼ to ½ cup butter substitute
lemon pepper to taste (2 tsp.)

Cut turnips into small chunks and boil in water until tender. Drain water from turnips. Place all ingredients in food processor and pulse until completely blended and the appearance of mashed potatoes. Add butter and lemon pepper.

Cauli-Bean Mash

Bob and I saw something like this on the Whole Foods buffet one day. Looking at the ingredients, we came home to create our own recipe. Later I saw an ad with a similar recipe using a popular salad dressing. I swapped it with my own **Ranch Dressing** *for a totally vegan dish.*

1 head of cauliflower
1 can chick peas/garbanzo beans
4 Tbsp. Earth Balance butter
Lemon pepper to taste
(Optional) **Vivian's Ranch Dressing**

Steam cauliflower and drain. Place beans in food processor and pulse. Add cauliflower, butter, and lemon pepper. Pulse again and blend. This is delicious as is, but, for a change, you may add **Vivian's Ranch Dressing**.

Cheese Grits Casserole

1 cup grits
3 cups water
1 package Daiya jalapeno cheese
1 package Daiya cheddar cheese
1 package frozen corn
1 cup sugar coated corn flakes
¼ cup melted Earth Balance spread

Boil grits in water for 5 minutes and let sit. Add cheeses and corn and continue to cook on medium heat until cheeses melt and blend with other ingredients. Pour into casserole dish and top with corn flakes to which melted spread has been added. Warm in oven at 350 degrees for 5-10 minutes. Freeze casserole without corn flake topping.

Creamed Spinach Over Pasta

Mother used to make this casserole with shrimp.

1 large onion
1 package fresh spinach
8oz. fresh mushrooms

1 to 2 Tbsp. nutmeg
1 pkg. seitan or 1 can white beans
3 Tbsp. Earth Balance spread
4 Tbsp. 100% whole wheat flour
1 cup vanilla almond milk
1 cup noodles

Sautee onion in a tablespoon of oil until golden. Add sliced mushrooms and spinach. Cook until tender. Set aside. Make white sauce by melting butter, adding flour until smooth, and then slowly adding milk while stirring. Season with nutmeg, and add vegetables plus seitan or beans. Serve over cooked noodles. May garnish with slivered almonds and serve with fruit or vegetable salad.

Gluten Free Mushroom Noodles

Several of my friends have difficult digestive systems requiring them to eat gluten and soy free diets. Wanting to invite them to our home for a meal and fellowship, I decided to experiment. The following is a result of my endeavors. Every ingredient is gluten free, soy free, and dairy free!

1 Tbsp. and 1 tsp. toasted sesame oil
8 ounces mushrooms, chopped
8 ounces gluten free corn spaghetti noodles (we use Sam Mills brand)
1 Tbsp. chopped basil
2-3 Tbsp. Earth Balance soy free butter substitute
(Optional) 1 can black beans, drained

Cook noodles in water until tender. Sautee mushrooms in 1 tablespoon oil until soft. Add 1 teaspoon oil to drained noodles and blend with rest of ingredients. Serve warm with a green vegetable like broccoli or asparagus and fruit salad to which you have added a tablespoon or two of local wildflower honey.

Grilled Vegetables

One of Bob's favorite finds was a closed wire basket made for grilling. It has a long double handle and opens to hold vegetables inside. Instead of turning the vegetables with a spatula, you just turn the basket over! **Grilled Vegetables** *serve as a delicious side dish or can be used in sandwiches or spaghetti. Be careful when grilling vegetables as each item cooks a little differently. You might have to turn the grill down a bit, cook to the side of the fire instead of in the center, or decrease your grill time.*

8oz. fresh mushrooms
2-3 yellow squash, sliced
2 to 3 leaves Bok Choy, cut into chunks
1 large onion, cut in slices
1 cup baby carrots
1 bell pepper, cut into bite-size pieces
¼ cup Worcestershire sauce
½ cup A1 sauce

Toss ingredients together and marinate for 1 hour or overnight. Place on hot grill and cook until soft and brown. Turn and grill on the other side. It normally takes about 10 to 15 minutes on each side, but be careful as vegetables can burn easily.

Jalapeno Mashed Sweet Potatoes

This is a quick and easy but delicious recipe, and it tastes great with your favorite green vegetable!

4 large sweet potatoes
¼ cup Earth Balance butter substitute
5 ounces Daiya Havarti Style Wedge:
    Jalapeno Garlic Cheese

Poke holes in potatoes with knife or fork for ventilation and bake in microwave for 8 minutes. Remove skins and mash. While still warm, add butter substitute and cheese and heat until melted. Mix well with potatoes.

Joan's Marinated Carrots

My mother earned her Home Economics degree from Madison College in Harrisonburg, Virginia, just up the street from where my father was raised! Mother could turn hot dogs into a fancy meal, especially with this side dish!

2 pounds carrots
1 small green pepper
1 medium onion
¾ cup red wine vinegar
10 ½ ounces tomato soup (or 1 cup catsup)
1 tsp. prepared mustard
(Optional) ¼ cup oil
1 tsp. Worcestershire sauce

1 cup sugar
1 teaspoon lemon pepper

Peel and slice carrots, cook until tender but not mushy. Add remaining ingredients and marinate over night.

Kale Medley

Kale has one of the highest scores on the ANDI (Aggregate Nutritional Density Index) scale but it can be tough to eat. To get the nutritional value, we add kale to salads or cook with onions. One day, I remembered a favorite dish of green beans, onions, and new potatoes and decided to try it with kale instead of green beans. We liked it! A year or so later, no potatoes on hand, Bob searched the pantry and found a can of hominy (a Southern corn). The results were delicious!

1 package of kale
1 large onion
6-8 small red potatoes (or 1 can hominy)
Mrs. Dash lemon pepper
Earth Balance butter substitute

Slice potatoes into quarters, slice onions into 1 inch chunks. Cook kale, onion, and potatoes in 4-6 cups water on high until soft enough for fork to pierce potatoes and onions are translucent. Drain and serve with butter substitute plus sprinkling of lemon pepper.

Potato Casserole

The original recipe came from my sister-in-law's cousin Donna. It is popular at all the Cate holiday functions. Using butter substitute, almond milk, vegan sour cream and cheese substitutes only enhances the flavor!

2 lb. frozen hash brown potatoes
¼ cup Earth Balance butter substitute
2 Tbsp. whole wheat flour
1 ¼ cup almond milk
1 can mushrooms or 8 ounces fresh mushrooms
2 Tbsp. butter substitute
1 chopped onion
1 pint (2 cups) Tofutti sour cream
1 ½ cup grated cheese alternative (8 ounces Daiya grated cheddar cheese)
½ cup butter substitute
2 cups frosted flakes

Defrost hash browns. Melt ¼ cup butter substitute in sauce pan, add flour and slowly blend in milk. Stir over medium heat until thickened. Add mushrooms.

Melt 2 Tbsp. butter substitute and combine with potatoes, onions, mushroom sauce, sour cream, and cheese. Pour into 3 quart casserole dish. Bake casserole at 350 degrees for 30 minutes.

Melt remaining ½ cup butter substitute and gently toss with corn flakes. Cover the heated casserole with corn flake mix and bake another 15 minutes. Serves an army (about 14) and can be frozen!

ADDITIONAL INFORMATION

Healthy Body, Healthy Soul

The Bible describes our bodies as temples of the Holy Spirit. While it is vital to feed our bodies with healthy plant-based foods, it is especially important to fill our souls with food that spiritually nurtures, strengthens, and guides us.

My life, like many of yours, has been a series of mountains and valleys. Sometimes those valleys have been horribly dark and frightening. Often I have felt overwhelmed, alone and abandoned. The Bible tells us that we *will* go through such trials. God even says He will never give us more than we can handle but will provide a way of escape. My answer to that is usually, "Yes, God, but don't You think Your estimation of me is a bit too high!" Not to disrespect my Lord, but that thought makes me laugh and then press back into His arms. That's the only safe place; my refuge and strength, my fortress is He ... not because of a religion, but because He has proven this many, many times during my 64 years of life.

The word of God is powerful. Just as plant based food provides nutrients that sustain physical health and help prevent disease, so God's word fills my spirit with truths that help me live and love like Father God while helping me overcome and endure trials. It is through God's word that I learn more about Him, find strength to help in time of need, get a picture of what Jesus did for me, realize Christ's forgiveness and grace, get direction for my life, gain a sense of peace in the midst of storms, and experience His unconditional love. God's word is the oil in my lamp, the sunshine on my garden, the afghan on a cold day, the energy drink before a game, the book that points me to truth.

God is my best friend. I share everything with Him, my joys and my concerns. He listens, He advises, He understands, He loves. He is always there. If you have never experienced a relationship with God the Father, I would like to share with you how that can happen.

First of all, God is holy. He cannot tolerate or even look upon sin. He is the one who created the earth and everything in it.

"In the beginning God created the heavens and the earth." (Genesis 1:1 NIV)

God *spoke* ...and there was light and darkness, water and sky, dry land and seas, vegetation, fruit trees, sun and moon, fish, birds, and land animals. Then God made Adam and Eve.

"God created mankind in his own image ... male and female he created them." (Genesis 1: 27 NIV)

But God had one rule. Don't eat of one particular tree. Adam and Eve had everything they could ever ask for ... food, friendship with Father God, a wonder-filled life ... but they disobeyed that one rule and sin came into the world. Therefore, ALL of us are sinners. It is in our genetic make-up.

For all have sinned and fall short of the glory of God (Romans 3:23 NIV)

Not only does sin separate us from the holy God, but it leads to lawlessness, chaos, hatred, murder, abuse and ... sin leads to destruction. God knew that, so He had to put a stop to sin.

The wages of sin is death (Romans 6:23a NIV)

The only thing that can truly satisfy us is a relationship with the Creator. Father wanted to restore that fellowship between man and God, so He sent His best, His Son Jesus, to live among us as God yet as man. Jesus Christ lived a perfect life, unlike anyone else has or will ever be able to do. He spent three years teaching us how to live God's way, a way of love and self-sacrifice, generously caring for one another and forgiving each other.

Then Jesus was taken before the governmental leaders of that day and sentenced to death. He was mocked and beaten, a crown of thorns was pressed onto His head, and He was crucified on a cross. Why? Because a blood sacrifice is the only way to atone for sin and bring us back into right relationship with Abba Father. Jesus said,

"I am the way and the truth and the life. No one comes to the Father except through Me." (John 14:6 NIV)

Jesus, in essence, stepped out in front of a speeding semi-truck and pushed us to safety. He took the punishment for my sin, for your sin, so that we can have ongoing fellowship with the Lord, with Father God.

For God so loved the world that he gave his one and only Son, that whoever believes in him shall not perish but have eternal life. (John 3:16 NIV)

What makes His death different from all others? He did not stay in the grave. He conquered death, came back to life and rose on the third day, and is now seated with the Father. Jesus said,

"I am the resurrection and the life. The one who believes in me will live, even though they die. (John 11:25 NIV)

But it does not stop there. Jesus is coming back to get His bride (those of us who believe in Him!)

Do not let your hearts be troubled. You believe in God, believe also in me. My Father's house many rooms; if that were not so, would I have told you that I am going there to prepare a place for you? And if I go and prepare a place for you, I will come back and take you to be with me that you also may be where I am. (John 14:1-3 NIV)

In the meantime, He sent the Holy Spirit to empower us to do what we cannot do on our own ... to live a righteous life with Abba Father.

"I will ask the Father, and he will give you another advocate to help you and be with you forever ... the Advocate, the Holy Spirit, whom the Father will send in my name, will teach you all things and will remind you of everything I have said to you. (John 14:16 25-26 NIV)

He who believes <u>has</u> eternal life (John 5:24). That means that this relationship is for all eternity, even after our physical death!

The gift of God is eternal life in Christ Jesus our Lord (Romans 6:23b NIV)

Would you like for God to walk with you through the mountains and valleys of this world, into eternity where there is no more disease, pain, sin? You can pray like this:

Father God, I am a sinner. I cannot save myself, but I believe that Jesus is Your Son and that He died to pay for my sin. He arose, conquering death once and for all, and He is now with You. I choose to follow You from this point forward. Teach me Your ways, Lord, and help me be obedient to Your will.

When you have surrendered your life to Christ, find a church to attend, begin a daily study of scripture (a One Year Bible study or reading one of the Gospels: Matthew, Mark, Luke, or John), talk to God throughout each day, and begin to share your faith with others! Meanwhile, remember that Father God loves YOU and has promised never to leave you nor forsake you!

Suggested Resources

Books:

The Engine 2 Diet by Rip Esselstyn. Published by Wellness Central, New York/Boston. ISBN 978-0-446-50669-4

The China Study by T. Colin Campbell, PhD and Thomas M. Campbell, II. Published by BenBella Books, Dallas, Texas. ISBN 978-1-932100-66-2

What the Bible says About Healthy Living by Rex Russell, M.D. Published by Fleming H. Revell, a Division of Baker Book House Co. in Grand Rapids, Michigan.

Online:

www.foodfacts.com
www.webmd.com
www.DrFuhrman.com
nutritiondata.self.com
ohsheglows.com/categories/recipes-2
www.livevegan.org/meatout-mondays

Other:

Forks Over Knives (a video), www.forksoverknives.com

<u>Nano Greens, Nano Reds, NanOmega, NanoPro, and EPA products</u> are researched, developed, and distributed by BioPharma Scientific, Inc., San Diego, CA 92121; for information

go to www.superfoodsolution.com (products must be ordered from a licensed medical professional).

Juice Plus: for information and research results or to order products, go to www.jcjpguy.com or contact Frank Zitzman, Physical Health Consultant, at 7242729315.

GROCERY LIST

PRODUCE	#	VEGAN	#	VEGAN	#	BREAD/CEREALS	#	CANNED	#
apples		Bacon,Smart Life		Milk, Almond Vanilla		Bread,Multigrain		applesauce	
bananas		Butter,EarthBalance		SourCrm,Toffutti		Buns,WheatBurger		beans, black	
cole slaw mix		Cheese,Daiya Block		Toturkey deli____		Buns,WheatHotDog		beans, chickpea	
carrots		Cheese,Daiya Shreds		Tofu		Cereal, UncleSam		beans, green/wax/lima	
celery		Cheese,Daiya Jalapeno		Yogurt, Soy		Cereal, WheatChex		beans, kidney	
garlic cloves		Cheese,Veggie PepperJack				Cereal,Bran		beans, pork &	
grapes		Chicken patties,Bocca				Crackers,WheatSaltn		cherries	
green peppers		Corn dogs				Crackers		fruit cocktail	
kale		CreamChs,Toffutti				Grits		oranges, mandarin	
lettuce, Romaine		EnerG Egg Replacer				Noodles,Macaroni		peaches/pears	
mushrooms,16oz.		Hot dogs		To Make Cheese		Noodles,Spaghetti		pineapple____	
onions		Hummus		AgarPowdr		Oatmeal		Salsa	
oranges		Ice Cream, Almond		CoconutOil		Pearl Barley		Sauerkrat, Bavarian	
potatoes, red/sweet		MeatCrumbls,Bocca		NutritionalYeast		Quinoa		spaghetti sauce	
squash____		Seiten		Onion Powder		Rice, Tex Mix		tomatoes, diced	
tomatoes		Soy sauce, Braggs		White Miso		Tortilla's		Water chestnuts	
BAKING GOODS	#	CONDIMENTS	#	PAPER GOODS	#	CLEAN SUPPLIES	#	FROZEN FOODS	#
Baking Pwdr (Al-free)		catsup		freezer tape		Comet		broccoli	
Baking Soda (Al-free)		mustard, Dijon/Regular		garbage bags, Glad		Detrgent,Clothes		brussels sprouts	
cake mix____		oil		kitty litter bags		Detrgent,Dish		corn	
extract____		olives, black/green		kleenex		Detrgnt,Dishwasher		green beans, thin	
Flour,WholeWheat		syrup: maple,panck		napkins		Ivory bar soap		juice, cranberry	
icing		PB/Jelly		paper plates		PineSol		juice, orange	
Mrs. Dash____		pickle relish		paper towel,Bounty		Shampoo/cream rinse		peas	
almnd/cashw/pecan/walnut		pickles, brd&butter		Seran wrap		Soft Scrub		sausage (Bocca links)	
spices____		Vegenaise		TP, Charmin		spray starch		spinach	
Sugar, Stevia		Vinegar,____		Ziplock (sz____)		toothpaste		strawberries,frozen	
Sunflower Seeds		Worchestershire		Ziplock (sz____)		Wipes, cleaning		vegies,mixed	

145

SAMPLE MONTHLY MEAL PLAN

	Beef-type meals	Soups	Variety	Chicken-type meals	Sandwiches	Variety
SUNDAY	MONDAY	TUESDAY	WEDNESDAY	THURSDAY	FRIDAY	SATURDAY
	Meatloaf w/ sauce	Vegie Soup	Stir Fry Spaghetti	Chicken Salad	Sub Sandwiches w/ Tofurkey & Vegies	Cream Vegies / Beans on Toast
	Mashed Potatoes	Cucumber Sandwich	Salad / Red Wine Dressing	Butternut Succotash	Peaches	Tossed Salad
	Tossed Salad		Garlic Toast	Green Beans		
SUNDAY	MONDAY	TUESDAY	WEDNESDAY	THURSDAY	FRIDAY	SATURDAY
	Spinach Burgers	Fagioli	Taco Salad	Sweet N Sour Chicken	Meatloaf Sandwich	Tomatoe Quiche
	Pineapple Coleslaw	Sweet Potato Muffins		Baked Summer Squash		Peas or Green Beans
	Jalop Mash Sw Potato	Assorted Fruit	Almond Bites	Broccoli w/ cheese	Grapes	Ambrosia
SUNDAY	MONDAY	TUESDAY	WEDNESDAY	THURSDAY	FRIDAY	SATURDAY
	Italian Sausage & Bean	Taco Soup	Oriental Stir Fry Veg	Cheesy Chkn Tort Stk	OLT Sandwiches	Blackeyed Pea Veg Cas
	Bavarian Kraut	Bob's Cornbread	Mandarin Quinoa Salad	Salad / Ranch Drsg.		Bob's Cornbread
	Mash Caulfl w/		Chinese Noodles		Apples	Pear / Peanut Butter
SUNDAY	MONDAY	TUESDAY	WEDNESDAY	THURSDAY	FRIDAY	SATURDAY
	Beef Cabbg Taco Cass	Broccoli Soup	Pot Pie	"Chicken" Burgers	Sausage in Blankets	Chicken Quesadillas
	Fruit Salad	Garlic Toast	Fruit Salad	Kale Medley		Cheese Grits Cass
		Salad / BBQ Drsg.		Peas	Bananas	Broccoli

MONTHLY MEAL PLAN

SUNDAY	MONDAY	TUESDAY	WEDNESDAY	THURSDAY	FRIDAY	SATURDAY
SUNDAY	MONDAY	TUESDAY	WEDNESDAY	THURSDAY	FRIDAY	SATURDAY
SUNDAY	MONDAY	TUESDAY	WEDNESDAY	THURSDAY	FRIDAY	SATURDAY
SUNDAY	MONDAY	TUESDAY	WEDNESDAY	THURSDAY	FRIDAY	SATURDAY